KING CHARLES III
A MODERN MONARCH

Written by Alison James

sona
BOOKS

sona
BOOKS

© Danann Media Publishing Limited 2023

First Published Danann Media Publishing Limited 2023

CAT NO: SON0562

Photography courtesy of

Getty images:

Tim Graham	Bettmann	Rolls Press
Anwar Hussein	Hulton Archive	WPA Pool
Fox Photos	Pool / Tim Graham Picture Library	Peter King
Hulton Deutsch	David Levenson	Evening Standard
Chris Jackson	Dave Benett	Tom Wargacki
Peter Nicholls	Mathieu Polak	Mathieu Polak
AFP	Richard Baker	Hugh R Hastings
Paul Popper / Popperfoto	Steve Back	UK Press Pool
Topical Press Agency	Max Mumby / Indigo	Picture Post
Stringer	Ray Bellisario	
Stanley Sherman	Mirrorpix	

All other images, Wiki Commons

Book cover design Darren Grice at Ctrl-d

Layout design Alex Young at Cre81ve

Copy Editor Juliette O'Neill

Made in EU.

ISBN: 978-1-915343-24-6

Contents

Introduction 8

A Boy born to be King 12

Prince of Wales 26

Action Man 38

Charlie's Angels 50

Diana 60

Camilla 72

Family Matters 84

Philanthropy, Passions, Projects and Pastimes 100

The Perpetual Prince 116

King Charles III 130

To Play a Prince 138

A King Crowned 140

Introduction

King Charles III will be the 40th monarch to be crowned in Westminster Abbey in a ceremony dating back almost a millennium. Life has changed beyond recognition in just the 70 years since his mother, Queen Elizabeth II, was crowned in June 1953 and, at a first glance, it is impossible to see how the ancient institution of monarchy can still exist in the 21st century. Rest assured, however, that in the form of this thoroughly modern and forward-thinking King — who has had to wait longer than any other heir apparent in British history to ascend the throne — it will not merely survive but thrive.

Below left:
The newly crowned Queen Elizabeth II waves to the crowd from the balcony at Buckingham Palace. Her son Prince Charles stands with her

Right:
King Charles III reacts during his visit to the newly built Guru Nanak Gurdwara, in Luton, north of London on December 6, 2022

Left:

King Charles III meets school children waving
flags during his visit to the newly built Guru
Nanak Gurdwara, in Luton, north of London on
December 6, 2022

A Boy born to be King

'He has large hands but fine with long fingers – quite unlike mine and certainly unlike his father's. It will be interesting to see what they will become. I still find it difficult to believe that I have a baby of my own'

The then Princess Elizabeth on examining her first baby, Charles, after his birth in November 1948

On the evening of November 14 1948, almost a year after the marriage of his parents - Princess Elizabeth of the United Kingdom and the Commonwealth, and Prince Philip, the Duke of Edinburgh - a 7lb 6oz baby Prince came into the world at Buckingham Palace in London. The ornate Buhl Room had been turned into a 'miniature hospital' for the occasion, with the Princess enduring a gruelling 33-hour labour which culminated in her giving birth by Caesarean section. The new father, who had occupied himself by playing squash and then going for a swim while he awaited news of the birth, was just towelling off when a footman rushed in and informed him the Princess had finally given birth. The Duke was at his wife's bedside when she came round from the anaesthetic and he presented her with a bouquet of red roses and carnations, having declared that his new born son resembled a *'plum pudding'*. Meanwhile, the King, George VI, so delighted that his heir and darling daughter had given birth to her own heir apparent, was heard cheering loudly as he entered the birthing suite. As tradition dictated, an announcement of the baby boy's birth was displayed on the railings of Buckingham Palace before the fountains of Trafalgar Square ran blue to in celebration. The next day, a 62 round gun salute thundered across the UK capital.

Right:

The future Queen Elizabeth II of England and Prince Philip of Edinburgh posing with their son Prince Charles

Below:

Well wishers waiting outside the gates of Buckingham Palace in London to hear the announcement of the birth of Prince Charles, 27th November 1948

At four-weeks-old, the baby prince was christened Charles Philip Arthur George beneath the ornate doom of the music room at Buckingham Palace. One of his eight godparents was his great grandmother Queen Mary.

'I gave the baby a silver gilt cup and cover which George III had given to a godson in 1780,' she wrote in her diary. *'I gave a present from my great grandfather to my great grandson 168 years later.'*

Delighted with her firstborn, Elizabeth breast-fed him for two months until she contracted measles and was forced to stop. Charles' babyhood was almost identical to that of his mother's some 22 years earlier — ie, very much in the hands of his nannies, Helen Lightbody and Mabel Anderson. His parents saw him for a spell in the mornings and evenings but the majority of the time was spent in the nursery with his Scottish carers. Indeed, his parents were absent for much of his early years. Not long after Charles had celebrated his first birthday, Elizabeth joined her husband at his naval posting in Malta over Christmas 1949, leaving their one-year-old son with his grandparents and nannies at Sandringham. His parents missed seeing his first steps and first teeth. When Prince Charles uttered his first word, it was *'Nana'* addressed to his nanny, whom he saw more of than any other person. He became a big brother when Princess Anne was born in August 1950 but as their mother was by now taking on extra royal duties due to the ill health of the King, the royal children saw less of her — and indeed their father who continued to pursue his naval career - than before.

It was the early death of George in February 1952 that brought the young couple back permanently to the United Kingdom, where Elizabeth acceded to the throne aged 25 while the Duke of Edinburgh resigned from the navy. Just 18 months after her accession, the new Queen was called upon to tour 13 countries over six months, without five-year-old Charles and three-year-old Anne. The Queen is said to have wept on bidding her children goodbye. The Queen Mother, who once more cared for Charles during his parents' tour, wrote to Elizabeth, *'You may find Charles much older in a very endearing way. He is intensely affectionate, and loves you and Philip most tenderly.'*

Left:
Prince Charles at five-weeks-old

Right:
Prince Charles is pushed around Green Park in his pram by his nanny on his second birthday

The two children were famously greeted with handshakes upon the return of their parents, though the Queen did dispense with some of the more formal traditions in that they were not required to bow or curtsey to their mother while young.

After two years of home-education with governess, Catherine Peebles, it was decided that shy and sensitive Charles attend school — the first heir to the British throne to do so. Both Queen Elizabeth and Prince Philip agreed that their children should not be hampered, neither socially nor educationally, by the constraints of home-schooling. Aged eight, Charles was sent boys-only pre-prep school Hill House in the Royal Borough of Kensington and Chelsea, London, arriving each day in a chauffeur-driven Rolls Royce. He attended the establishment for just six months but appeared to enjoy his time there. A school report from the time remarked that he was 'determined but slow with above-average intelligence' and 'full of go, full of physical courage… a damned good lad.'

In September 1957, Charles was moved to Cheam Preparatory School in Headley, Hampshire — the oldest prep school in the country which had first opened its doors in 1645. His father had previously been a pupil there. Now a boarder, the young prince was homesick to begin with — not helped by the fact that he was bullied for his 'jug' ears - and would write home each week, informing his parents of the fact.

'Charles is just beginning to dread the return to school next week–so much worse for the second term,' the Queen wrote to Prime Minister Anthony Eden at the beginning of January 1958.

Left:

Princess Elizabeth with her husband, Prince Philip, and their children Prince Charles and the baby Princess Anne

Right:

Prince Charles wearing his uniform for Cheam School in 1959

He went on to find an outlet, however, in school drama productions and also by trying his hardest at cricket, football and rugby. He became the head boy in his final year by which time conversations were being had about the next step in his educational journey. His beloved granny, The Queen Mother, was strongly in favour of Charles attending Eton College, the ancient boarding school near Windsor Castle. In a letter to the Queen in May 1961, the Queen Mother described Eton as 'ideal . . . for one of his character & temperament.'

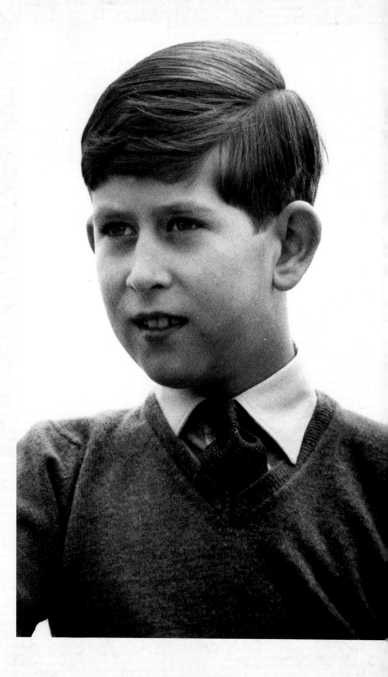

Prince Philip, however, had other ideas and was adamant his son attend Philip's own alma mater, Gordonstoun, located in an isolated part of north eastern Scotland. The school — which championed physical and mental fortitude and whose motto is 'There Is More In You' — was intended to toughen Charles up, something Philip badly felt he needed. Students took cold showers, slept on hard beds and went on morning runs before breakfast, whatever the weather. The Queen sided with her husband and thus it was to Gordonstoun that Charles went. He was later to describe the school as 'Colditz with kilts', likening it to the infamous World War II Prisoner of War camp in Nazi Germany. While the school had suited Philip's assertive, brusque personality and prowess as a sportsman, it did not suit sensitive, artistic and already philosophical Charles. He was singled out as a victim and bullied from day one, plus his titles and status as heir to the throne made him a natural target in a school, later described by one of the prince's classmates as being a place where 'bullying was virtually institutionalized and very rough - I never saw him (Charles) react at all. He was very stoic. He never fought back.'

It was while Charles was at Gordonstoun that he made headlines — but for all the wrong reasons. In June 1963 when he was 14, he was sailing around the Isle of Lewis with the school and, once landed at Stornoway Harbour, was taken to a pub — something which would never happen today. He promptly ordered a cherry brandy.

'I said the first drink that came into my head,' he recalled, 'because I'd drunk it before, when it was cold, out shooting.'

As fate would have it, a tabloid newspaper reporter also happened to be in the hostelry with the result that the story went around the world. Afterwards, his friendly, supportive police body guard, Don Green, was sacked. Charles was inconsolable. Green had become like a father figure to him.

'I have never been able to forgive them for doing that,' he was later to say. 'I thought it was the end of the world.'

The arts and music became something of a refuge for Charles while at Gordonstoun. Having been with his grandmother, The Queen Mother, to see a concert with celebrated cellist Jacqueline du Pré, he was inspired to take up the instrument. A new English teacher at the school reawakened his passion for the theatre and in 1965, the prince played Macbeth. His parents came to see the performance, which his father ruined by laughing loudly at his son's acting. When Charles later asked why Philip had laughed, the insensitive Duke replied, 'It sounded like The Goons'.

Charles did not excel on the sports field. He did however become a skilled fisherman and shot. He also took up his father's sport — polo — and proved to be a formidable player. When he was 17, Charles took time out from Gordonstoun

---

Left:

Back to school and fully recovered from his recent tonsilectomy, eight year old Prince Charles (Center) goes out June 7th 1957 for a recreational period walk with some of his class mates escorted by an unidentified schoolmistress. The Prince, a day boy at Kensingston school, will spend the weekend with the royal family at Windsor

Right:

Gordonstoun School logo with the motto 'Plus est en vous' which translates to 'There Is More In You'

PLUS EST   EN VOUS

to spend two terms at Timbertop School in the mountains near Melbourne, Australia. His father thought the experience would be beneficial — and, for once with regards to Charles' education, Philip made the right decision. The young prince took to Timbertop like a duck to proverbial water. The onus was on the outdoors and taught students a curriculum focusing on gruelling hikes, cross-country runs, skiing, solo camping trials and woodcutting. Charles found himself relishing each and every challenge. Students and masters alike immediately made him feel at home and were interested in the kind of person he was rather than who he was.

'Quite frankly, it was by far the best part of my education,' he was later to remark. *'While I was there, I had the pommy bits bashed off me. Like chips off an old block.'*

Charles returned to Gordonstoun in the autumn of 1966 for his final year and was made head boy or 'Guardian' in Gordonstoun parlance. Despite having once called the school *'a prison*

sentence', Charles later said, *'I believe it taught me a great deal about myself and my own abilities and disabilities. It taught me to accept challenges and take the initiative.'*

From Gordonstoun, in another break with royal tradition, Charles went to Cambridge University in September 1967 rather than join the British Armed Forces. His arrival at Trinity College had all the appearances of a welcome given to a pop star. Over 1000 sightseers and well-wishers gathered at the gates of the college and their screams drowned out the words of greeting from Lord Butler, Master of Trinity. He read Archaeology and Anthropology before changing to History for the second part of his degree and was awarded a 2:2 in 1970.

Before he graduated, however, his royal destiny would take centre stage. Although he had formally been declared Prince of Wales, aged 10, in 1958, it was decided that the investiture ceremony should take place at Caernarfon Castle, north Wales, some years hence. The date agreed on was July 1 1969.

Left:

Prince Charles (centre back) with his family in 1965

Below:

Trinity College Great Court

Left:

Prince Charles sits on the floor with unidentified fellow students during a rehearsal of his college dramatic society at Cambridge in 1969

Above:

Coat of arms of Trinity College, Cambridge

Prince of Wales

'I, Charles, Prince of Wales, do become your liege man of life and limb and of earthly worship, and faith and truth I will bear unto thee to live and die against all manner of folks'

Oath made by Prince Charles at his investiture as Prince of Wales, July 1 1969

The title of Prince of Wales is one that has traditionally been bestowed to the male heir apparent of the English or British monarch, since King Edward I of England gave his son, Edward of Caernarfon, the title in 1284. The bestowal is neither automatic nor hereditary. Edward the younger was born in Caernafon Castle

in 1284 — the location was possibly chosen by Edward I as a deliberate statement to the recently conquered Welsh. The Prince of Wales title came with the royal lands in Wales, as well as the title Earl of Chester. The first Prince of Wales spent five weeks in Caernarfon in 1301 but never returned. After rising against the English, native Welshman Owain Glyndwr proclaimed himself Prince of Wales in 1400 but, since his defeat in 1409, the title has reverted to a ceremonial one, given to male heirs apparent of the English throne. As previously stated, Queen Elizabeth II made her eldest son, Charles, Prince of Wales in July 1958. He was the 21st to be given the title. Elizabeth's uncle Edward or David as he was known, the future King Edward VIII, had been the previous Prince of Wales and was invested at Caernarfon Castle in 1911 before becoming King in 1936. The 1911 ceremony had been a new invention, using medieval symbolism, which would be repeated with Charles' investiture on July 1 1969.

In preparation for his investiture as Prince of Wales, or 'Tywysog Cymru' as the title was known in Welsh, Charles was taken out of Cambridge for a term and sent to the University of Aberystwyth in order to prepare for his role and study the Welsh language under

the tutelage of Dr Tedi Millward, a fervent Welsh Nationalist. The Prime Minister of the time, Harold Wilson hoped it would promote a spirit of unity between England and Wales. However, many Welsh people were deeply unhappy that an English-born man would once again assume the role of Prince of Wales and Charles' arrival met with opposition.

'Every day I had to go down to the town where I went to these lectures, and most days there seemed to be a demonstration going on against me,' he was later to say. *'Usually by splendid middle-aged ladies who got out of a bus. That was an interesting experience. I did my utmost to learn as much Welsh as I could which in a term it is quite difficult and I am not as brilliant a linguist as I would like to be. But my being there for that period it did make an enormous difference to my understanding of the way Wales works and what I did pick up particularly was an immense sense of real community. It is a wonderful mosaic that I think makes the principality so*

Left:

The coronet of Charles, Prince of Wales (1969) on display at the Victoria and Albert Museum, London, in 2012

Above:

Caernarfon Castle

Right:

A section of a protest against the investiture outside the castle in March 1969

special. One of the great special memories I have of being at Aberystwyth of that term was the opportunity it gave me to explore so much of that remarkable part of Wales and Cardiganshire, as it then was. I remember on one occasion driving about, it must have been somewhere above Cors Caron, where I got completely and utterly lost. There was nobody about at all until finally this splendid figure on a bicycle appeared. We stopped him, and, trying to deploy what Welsh I had learnt from Dr Millward, I tried to find out where I was.'

It was this positive, can-do attitude that saw him making friends rather than enemies. Against the odds, the prince won the majority of his detractors round — including Dr Millward.

'I was a well-known nationalist, so I was a little surprised when the university asked me if I would teach Welsh to Prince Charles

Above:

Pupils Ian Graves and Julie Radford admire the mugs presented by Cardiff City Council to children at Bryn Hafod Junior School, Llanrumney, Cardiff. These are to commemorate the Investiture of Prince Charles, 26th June 1969

Right:

View from Caernarfon Castle across the town square at the gathered crowds for the Investiture of Prince Charles, 01 July, 1969

for a term,' he said in a 2015 interview. *'He had a one-on-one tutorial with me once a week. He was eager, and did a lot of talking. By the end, his accent was quite good.'*

Dr Millward's daughter, Llio, has spoken of her father's hopes for tutoring Charles.

'He hoped it was an opportunity to enlighten an important member of the English organization about the cause of the language,' she said.

When Dr Millward passed away in 2020 at the age of 89, the Prince of Wales expressed his condolences.

'I am deeply saddened to hear of Dr Millward's death. I have very fond memories of my time in Aberystwyth with Dr Millward over 51 years ago,' he pronounced. *'While I am afraid I might not have been the best student, I learned an immense amount from him about the Welsh language and about the history of Wales. After all these years, I am forever grateful to him for helping foster my deep and abiding love for Wales, her people and her culture.'*

Below:

Pictured on their way to the investiture, Prince Charles and Princess Anne, Caernarfon, Wales, 1st July 1969

Right:

Prince Charles kneels before the Queen during the ceremony of his investiture as Prince of Wales at Caernarfon Castle, Gwynedd, Wales, 1st July 1969. On the queen's left is Prince Philip. The ceremony is taking place on a dais with a perspex canopy and a circular plinth in Welsh slate

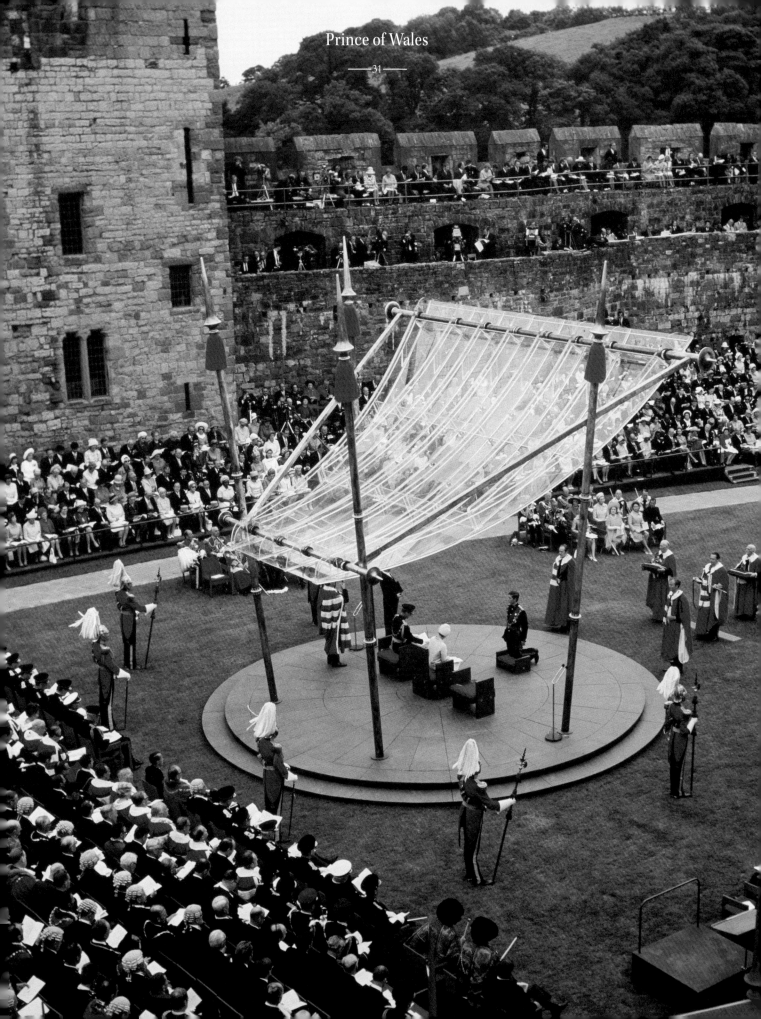

The investiture, which was two years in the planning, was preceded by a year-long promotional campaign, known as 'Croeso '69' (Welcome '69, in English), which, it was hoped, would raise the profile of Wales and promote tourism. Charles' uncle, photographer and designer Lord Snowdon, the then husband of Princess Margaret, designed the ceremony and arranged for it to be TV-friendly. The ceremony took place on a circular late dais shielded by a large modern canopy of perspex which allowed the audience and television cameras to watch the proceedings. The investiture was designed to celebrate both the pride in Wales and the British monarchy.

For an hour prior to the arrival of the royal family on the big day, a procession of dignitaries and guests paraded through the town of Caernarfon and entered the castle through the Water Gate, led by the Queen's heralds with a guard of honour of the Welsh Guards. Several dozen teenagers followed, representing Welsh youth. Then came the invited members of the House of Lords, the members and aldermen of Caernarfon Borough Council, members of the Gorsedd (the society of Welsh-language poets, writers, musicians and others who had contributed to the Welsh language and to public life in Wales), the National Eisteddfod Court, chairmen of the 13 Welsh county councils, county sheriffs and the Welsh MPs. Church representatives arrived, then Prime Minister, Harold Wilson and his wife Mary, the Home Secretary James Callaghan and the chiefs of staff of the armed forces. Members of the royal family arrived in a fleet of four cars, led by the Lord Lieutenant of Caernarfonshire. Finally, Charles — who was, according to Lord Snowdon, *'s**t scared'* - made his entrance in an open carriage accompanied by his equerry and the Secretary of State for Wales to the accompaniment of a rendition of 'God Bless the Prince of Wales' by the Band of the Welsh Guards.

In front of the invited audience of 4,000 people inside the castle, Charles came to the stage and knelt on a scarlet cushion. The Secretary of State for Wales read the Letters Patent in Welsh as the Queen draped an ermine-covered, purple velvet cloak around her son's shoulders, handed him a golden rod, a mantle, a sword, a girdle, and a ring.

'My mama was busy dressing me, rather like she did when I was small,' he remarked years later.

She then crowned him with a gold coronet adorned with diamonds set in platinum which had been specially made for the occasion and was a gift from the Worshipful Company of Goldsmiths to the Queen. Unable to source a suitable orb for the top of the coronet, a ping-pong ball spray-painted gold and engraved with the Prince of Wales' insignia was finally settled upon. The coronet used at the investiture of the future Edward VIII in 1911 had mysteriously gone missing, hence the necessity for a new one. Interestingly, after the death of the Duke of Windsor - the former Edward VIII - in 1972, the old coronet was found amongst his possessions.

The prince then placed his hands between his mother's and took the oath.

'I, Charles, Prince of Wales, do become your liege man of life and limb and of earthly worship and faith and truth I will bear unto thee to live and die against all manner of folks,' he announced.

Left:

Queen Elizabeth II crowns her son Charles, Prince of Wales, during an investiture ceremony at Caernarfon Castle

Below:

Prince Charles, wearing the gold coronet looks on at his investiture as Prince of Wales

He was later to say that this had been the most meaningful and moving part of the ceremony for him.

The prince kissed his mother on the cheek before she led him to the balcony of the Queen's Gate to greet the crowds waiting outside the castle. He later sat himself on a throne, between two further thrones occupied by the Queen to one side and his father, the Duke of Edinburgh, sitting to the other side.

The ceremony was broadcast live on BBC television from 10.30am till 4.30pm. It was also broadcast on BBC Radio 3 and bilingually on BBC Radio 4 Wales. It had an audience of 19 million in the UK and 500 million worldwide. Though 250,000 visitors were predicted for Caernarfon, only about 90,000 visited the town to see the event for themselves. It was believed many people chose to watch the ceremony at home on television instead.

Following the event, Charles spent four days touring Wales by car, helicopter and The Royal Yacht 'Britannia'. Leaving the royal yacht in Llandudno the day after the investiture (and rejoining at various points on the trip), the Prince visited Newtown, New Quay, St Davids, Gelli Aur, Llanelli, Swansea, Merthyr Tydfil, Newport and Cardiff. He ended the tour with a presentation at the City Hall and a concert at the New Theatre. Charles was said to be *'utterly amazed'* by the support he had received from large crowds during the tour and by the way the Welsh people had decorated the streets in his honour. On his return to Windsor Castle, he wrote in his diary that it seemed *'very odd'* not having to wave to hundreds of people.

Left:

Queen Elizabeth II presents Prince Charles to the people of Wales at Queen Eleanor's Gate Caernarfon Castle, 1st July 1969

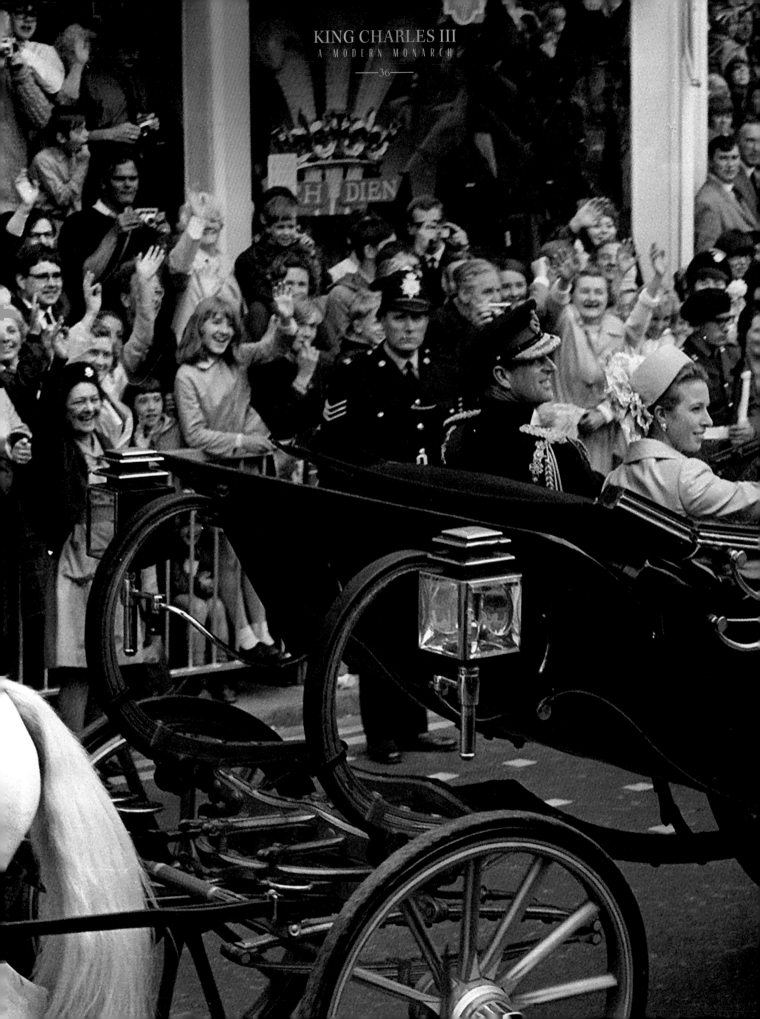

Above:

Prince Charles with his sister Princess Anne and his parents Queen Elizabeth II and Prince Phillip, Duke of Edinburgh, making his way by carriage from Caernarfon Castle, where he was invested as the Prince Of Wales, 1st July 1969

Action Man

'I don't know how Charles survived his life in the navy. He was not made for a commodore's life. The private person was too strong and he couldn't enter into the spirit of the service'

Charles' cousin, Lady Pamela Hicks

The Military

In a tradition going back centuries, male Royal heirs have always spent time in the military. Prince Charles was no different. During his second year at Cambridge, he requested and received Royal Air Force training, learning to fly the Chipmunk aircraft with Cambridge University Air Squadron. In March 1971, he began training as a jet pilot at the Royal Air Force college at Cranwell in Lincolnshire — having flown himself there following RAF training he had received while at Cambridge. Charles was initially reluctant about the joining the RAF but was persuaded to do so by his father. His training was condensed into five months rather than the standard year. As it turned out he loved flying jets — even if the technical, mathematical side of things didn't come easily to him — and he spoke of feeling *'power, smooth, unworried power'* when he flew solo. He was presented with his RAF wings in a passing out ceremony in August 1971.

Following in the footsteps of his father, grandfather, great uncle Lord Mountbatten and two of his great-grandfathers, Charles then embarked on a naval career and enrolled in a six-week course at the Royal Naval College, Dartmouth. As at Cranwell, the technical side of things — specifically navigation - were problematic for him. He is even said to have fallen asleep in one class. Neither did it do much for his confidence to know that both

his father and great uncle had distinguished themselves in this area. The prince began his active service on the guided missile destroyer HMS Norfolk from 1971-72, followed by time spent on the frigates HMS Minerva from 1972-3 and HMS Jupiter in 1974. He was not a natural fit for the Navy and on one occasion wrote to Mountbatten about his *bouts of hopeless depression* because he felt unable to cope. Later that year, Charles joined the Royal

Naval Air Station, Yeovilton where he trained as a helicopter pilot. Upon qualifying, he was assigned to 845 Naval Air Squadron on board the commando carrier HMS Hermes. In February 1976, Charles took command of the coastal minehunter HMS Bronington for his last ten months of active service by which time he had been made a commander. In 1978, he took part in a parachute training course at RAF Brize Norton, having been appointed colonel-in-chief of the Parachute Regiment the year before. However, while he had experience parachuting, the first time he tried it he got stuck upside down in the rigging. He had not completed the Army's parachutist training course and felt he could not '*look them in the eye*' nor wear the Parachute Regiment's famous beret and wings badge unless he had done the course. So, he asked to do so and subsequently completed it.

Despite leaving the military, the prince continued to work closely with the Armed Forces. Charles does not have any medals for active service in a war - rather for serving in a particular location, being a member of a high-ranking order or being awarded medals from other nations.

The former Prince of Wales, now King, can be seen wearing the following medals; Queen's Service Order (New Zealand), Coronation Medal, Silver Jubilee Medal, Golden Jubilee Medal, Diamond Jubilee Medal, Naval Long Service Good Conduct (LSGC), Canadian Forces Decoration, the New Zealand Commemorative Medal, and the New Zealand Armed Forces Award. In 2012, Queen Elizabeth II awarded him the highest rank in all three services - Field Marshal, Admiral of the Fleet and Marshal of the Royal Air Force.

Left:

The Prince of Wales, receives his wings at RAF Cranwell in Lincolnshire, UK, 20th August 1971. On the right is his father, the Duke of Edinburgh (1921 - 2021), who is Marshal of the Royal Air Force

Right:

Charles completing his Parachute training as Colonel-in-Chief of the Parachute Regiment at RAF South Cerney, 25th April 1978

Sporting Hero

'Charles, I think, enjoyed playing polo very, very much. I think he wanted to prove to his father that he could do what his father could and was a very good person to play with' — Polo legend Paul Withers who was on the first all-English team to win the Gold Cup with Prince Philip in 1968.

For a great deal of his adult life, Charles was a keen and competitive polo player. He became interested in polo as a child, watching his father, The Duke of Edinburgh, play at Windsor, and it was the Duke who bought him his first polo pony. In his early teens, the Prince played practice chukkas (a period of time in polo) at Windsor during the school holidays. He played his first game in 1963 aged 15, in a team captained by The Duke of Edinburgh and he played his first game in public in April 1964. From then on, the Prince played as regularly as he could

manage, playing his first season of first class games in 1967. His handicap rose gradually from one in 1967 to four in 1982. The main grounds on which the Prince played were Smith's Lawn in Windsor Great Park, Cowdray Park in Sussex and Cirencester Park, Gloucestershire. Prince Charles also played polo during visits to countries including Australia, India, the USA, France, Brazil, Kenya, Malta and Ghana. He played in many teams, including Cambridge University whilst an undergraduate, when he won his half-Blue playing against Oxford; for the Royal Navy; and in more recent years with Les Diables Bleus and the Maple Leaf. He often played with sons William and Harry in the Highgrove team. Charles played in all four positions but usually No 4 (back). He regularly played to raise money for charity — for instance, during 2005/6, he raised £900,000 taking the total over the previous 11 years to £8.4 million. In June 1990, the Prince broke his arm in two places when he fell from his pony during a match at Cirencester Park. His Royal Highness was able to return to the game the following April and played regularly up until his decision to retire in November 2005. While he may no longer play, the new King maintains his interest in the sport.

The then Prince of Wales took his first skiing lessons at the age of 14, in January 1963, when he was staying with Prince Ludwig of Hesse at Tarasp in Switzerland. The young Prince went on to enjoy skiing holidays, taking trips to Liechtenstein in 1965 and near Davos, Switzerland, in 1966. Over the years, Charles continued to take annual skiing holidays with his sons, usually

Left:

Prince Philip, Duke of Edinburgh, takes a break from the polo match to chat with his son Prince Charles and daughter Princess Anne June 1956

Right:

Prince Charles playing polo for Windsor Park, on May 16, 1982, at Ham Polo Club in Ham, Surrey

visiting Klosters in Switzerland. Like it has for many, skiing has greatly impacted the Prince's life, bringing both joy and sadness. It provided an escape for him but the mountains both gave and took from him. In 1988 two members of his party, Mrs. Palmer-Tomkinson and Major Hugh Lindsay, were swept away in an avalanche. It was then that Princess Diana vowed never to ski again. At the time, the Major's wife was pregnant. Mrs Palmer-Tomkinson was severely injured but tragically Major Lindsay was killed.

The Prince took up water-skiing and surfing in his teens, and during service in the Royal Navy he was introduced to aqua-lung diving. In 1974, he became President of the British Sub Aqua Club. In July 1975, he spent 47 minutes under water examining the wreck of the Mary Rose, a Tudor warship sunk off Portsmouth in 1545 — making him the first member of the Royal Family to see it since Henry VIII watched the ship sink. It was the first of a number of dives Charles made to the wreck, and he became President of the Mary Rose Trust which raised the remains of the ship in 1982 for preservation in a new museum at Portsmouth.

Above:

Prince Charles, the President of the Mary Rose Trust, puts on a wetsuit in preparation for diving to see the Tudor Shipwreck which sank in the Solent in 1545, Portsmouth, 28th April 1982

Right:

Prince Charles With Prince William And Prince Harry On A Skiing Holiday In Klosters, Switzerland in 1994

Charles enjoyed sailing from early childhood, taking part in his first yacht race at Cowes Regatta with his father, The Duke of Edinburgh, at the age of eight. In 1978, he windsurfed off the Isle of Wight during another visit to the Cowes Regatta. In 1979 HRH was given a skateboard for Christmas and after practising at Windsor, was able to give a brief demonstration for a television news programme about a North London community organisation. Viewers saw Charles ask a startled youngster, *'Can I borrow your board?'*

Charles is an accomplished horseman and in the 1980s, rode in a number of competitive races. He made his debut as a jockey in 1980 at a charity race at Plumpton, East Sussex. He came second on 'Long Wharf' in the two-mile Madhatters' Private Stakes on that March — his horse was 13-8 favourite. Four days later at Sandown, Charles rode in his first steeplechase, the Duke of Gloucester Memorial Trophy hunter chase. HRH rode

Above:

Prince Charles Windsurfing In Deauville, France in 1978

Right:

Prince Charles jumping a fence on the Steeplechase Course at Sandown Park, 1980

'Sea Swell' for Lambourn trainer Nick Gaselee, finishing fourth. The Prince, familiar with jumping in the show ring, cross country team events and polo, bought his first racehorse in May 1980 - 'Allibar', a 10-year-old bay gelding. In one race, in October 1980, at Ludlow, Shropshire, he came second in a field of 12. Sadly, 'Allibar' died of a heart attack in February 1981. That year Charles bought 'Good Prospect', a 12-year-old bay gelding who was also a steeplechaser. The Prince rode him twice, in the Grand Military Gold Cup at Sandown on March 13, and in the Kim Muir Memorial Challenge Cup at Cheltenham four days later - but fell on both occasions. On 21st May 1981, The Prince rode in his last race, at Newton Abbot, Devon, on Queen Elizabeth The Queen Mother's horse Upton Grey, finishing ninth. The Prince's racing colours were scarlet with royal blue sleeves and black cap. In summarising his racing career, Nick Gaselee, The Prince's former trainer,

said Charles had not been credited over the years for his racing achievements.

'*To come in the top four in his first three races is a record any professional jockey would be proud of,*' said Gaselee, '*and that is despite his many other commitments at that time.*'

Charles has also hunted to hounds but no longer does so.

Fly fishing is another outdoor passion which he shared with his late grandmother and father. He has also taught his sons how to use a rod. Charles has been a sharp salmon fisherman since youth, enjoying the sport as often as he can on Royal Deeside in the Highlands of Scotland. So keen is he that he has been known to extend his stays at Balmoral because the fishing is so good.

Right:

Prince Charles Fishing For Salmon In The River Dee, Balmoral in 1982

Charlie's Angels!

'Thirty is a good age to get married'

Prince Charles comments on matrimony in 1975, aged 27

This was a quotation that the Prince would live to regret ever having uttered. The future king had been reportedly advised by his great uncle, Lord Louis Mountbatten to '*sow his wild oats and have as many affairs as he could*' while he was young. But as the world's most eligible bachelor, no sooner would Charles have started dating a girl than the world's press were hearing wedding bells. His string of romances resulted in his girlfriends being dubbed '*Charlie's Angels*'.

In a 1969 interview, Charles spoke about the huge pressure his future role put him under, explaining to journalists, '*You've got to remember when you marry, in my position, you're going to marry someone who perhaps one day will become Queen. You've got to choose somebody very carefully, I think, who can fulfil this particular role, because people like you, perhaps, would expect quite a lot from somebody like that, and it's got to be somebody pretty special.*'

By 1976 - a year after he had made the remark about 30 being the right age to marry - the question of who and when Prince Charles would wed had become a matter of national preoccupation. At the age of 28, having completed his naval service, the Prince was also beginning to consider more seriously the constitutional need for him to find a wife. His situation, however, like much of his earlier life, was complicated by his

position. As he had remarked seven years earlier, he was required not only to find a wife, a woman with whom he could happily share his life, but someone who could one day undertake the role of Queen. Both the country and the Family were growing increasingly eager to see the royal 'action man' joined in holy matrimony.

According to royal experts, the Prince had more than 20 romantic liaisons over the 13 years between 1967 and 1980, the year he met Lady Diana Spencer, the future Princess of Wales. Some women such as American heiress Laura Jo Watkins and actress Susan George were quick flings while others were more serious. The following fall into this latter category. . .

Lucia Santa Cruz

Charles met the daughter of the former Chilean ambassador to London in the late 1960s when he was studying at Cambridge. They are said to have met at a dinner party hosted by a mutual friend. At five years older than the prince, Lucia was, according

Right:

Chilean historian Lucia Santa Cruz, the former girlfriend of Prince Charles, UK, 21st August 1973

to Charles' cousin Lady Elizabeth Anson, *'the first real love of his life'*. The prince was widely known to be shy and socially awkward but still his relationship with Lucia progressed. The Master of Trinity College, Rab Butler, is said to have given Lucia a key to his lodge so the couple could meet in private. Charles and Lucia were photographed in London in the back seat of a chauffeur-driven car and it's thought that Charles even took Lucia to Balmoral to meet the family. Lucia is credited with not only being Charles' first sexual partner but also the person who introduced him to perhaps the most important woman in his life — the then Camilla Shand. While no one quite knows why things between Lucia and Charles ended, what we do know is that by 1971 she had moved into a flat in the London suburb of Belgravia. Living in the apartment below was debutante Camilla Shand and the two women became firm friends with Lucia introducing Charles to Camilla. Lucia married politician Juan Luis Ossa with whom she had three children. She remained friends with Charles and Camilla until her death in March 2019.

Camilla Shand

The daughter of a British Army officer whose great-grandmother, Alice Keppel, was a mistress of King Edward VII, Camilla and Charles reportedly courted for six months after Charles pursued her with *'elaborately worded love notes'* and late-night telephone chats. They broke up in 1972 when Charles left the UK to serve on a Royal Navy frigate. When he returned after eight months, Camilla was engaged to her on-and-off-again boyfriend, British army lieutenant Andrew Parker Bowles, whom she married in 1973. It is thought that senior Royals breathed a collective sigh of relief when Camilla tied the knot with Parker Bowles. It has even been suggested that the Queen Mother met both Camilla and

Left:

Charles chats to Camilla at a polo match, circa 1972

Below:

Lady Jane Wellesley, daughter of The Duke of Wellington, watching Charles at Quorn Hunt cross country event

Andrew's parents in order to broker the deal. The reason? It has been mooted that the Royals wanted Charles to marry someone with the highest aristocratic pedigrees plus, and perhaps more importantly, it was public knowledge that Camilla had had proper relationships before Charles and also Andrew Parker Bowles. Camilla couldn't put up any pretence of purity. Unfortunately, those around Charles believed it was important that his wife – and future queen – not have an extensive romantic history. True love will out, though, and, as we all know, Charles and Camilla ended up together after many years apart.

Lady Jane Wellesley

The infinitely suitable daughter of the 8th Duke of Wellington, and the Prince of Wales dated between 1973-74 when Lady Jane was in her early 20s and was considered to be a key candidate for marriage. Intense media scrutiny was blamed for their split, although perhaps this wasn't the real reason. When once asked if there was to be an engagement announcement, Jane replied: 'Do you honestly believe I want to be Queen?'. A film producer and author, Lady Jane has never married.

Davina Sheffield

In 1976, the prince fell for Davina Sheffield, granddaughter of the first Lord McGowan and the cousin of former British Prime Minister David Cameron's wife, Samantha. They were introduced by Charles' sister, Princess Anne. Davina seemed ideal in many ways but she already had a boyfriend when Charles met her, an Old Harrovian and powerboat racer named James Beard. Davina initially rebuffed invitations to have dinner with the Prince, but he was so persistent that she eventually succumbed and the boyfriend soon fell by the wayside. Rumours began circulating that Charles was going to propose but then Beard was conned into talking about his

Above:

Davina Sheffield, wearing a riding hat, attends the Cotswold Hunt cross country riding event, location unspecified, in the Cotswolds, Gloucestershire, England, 21st October 1979

relationship with Davina by what turned out to be a Sunday tabloid reporter and the story of their affair, complete with photographs of their 'love nest', made headline news. It killed Davina and Charles' blossoming relationship stone dead. Davina went on to marry Jonathan Derek Morley in 1981, the same year Charles married Diana. The couple had three sons together and remain married.

Lady Sarah Spencer

The eldest daughter of the 8th Earl Spencer, and big sister of Princess Diana, started dating her future brother-in-law in 1977. It was not a long relationship and Charles and Sarah split up early in 1978 after she spoke about their relationship to the press. She reportedly told 'Time' magazine, 'There is no chance of my marrying him. I'm not in love with him. And I wouldn't marry anyone I didn't love whether he were the dustman or the King of England'. Sarah went on to marry Lincolnshire farmer Neil McCorquodale in 1980. The couple have three children - Emily, George, and Celia. While many might feel strange about their younger sister going on to date — and marry - their ex-boyfriend, Sarah reportedly took pride in the fact that she set Charles and Diana up. 'I introduced them,' she once said. 'I'm Cupid'.

Below:

Prince Charles sitting next to Lady Sarah Spencer at a polo match in 1977

Sabrina Guinness

Charles started dating brewing dynasty heiress and society 'It Girl', Sabrina in 1979. Charles was said to be besotted with her and took her to Balmoral to meet the family. They went to the polo and theatre together and she pointedly took fly-fishing lessons as it was one of Charles's favourite hobbies. Princess Margaret described the relationship as *'serious'* but Charles was said to drop her suddenly after nine months as The Queen was unhappy with her *'racy'* past. She was always said to be the *'liveliest'* of Charles' girlfriends. After her relationship with Charles, Sabrina went on to date a string of A-listers from Mick Jagger to David Bowie. Being *'Charles' ex'* labelled her for 34 years until 2014 when she married acclaimed playwright, Sir Tom Stoppard.

Right:

Sabrina Guinness with Charles at the Guards Polo Club in 1981

Below:

Lady Amanda Knatchbull, the Granddaughter of Earl Mountbatten was tipped as a bride for Prince Charles in the 1970s

Lady Amanda Knatchbull

It was a long-held ambition of Lord Mountbatten that his granddaughter, Lady Amanda Knatchbull, would marry Prince Charles. The two had known each other for years, although Amanda was nine years Charles' junior. They briefly became an item shortly before Mountbatten's death in 1979. Amanda had become fond of Charles, liking his energy, enthusiasm, sense of fun, kindness and modest self-deprecation. Sensible and loving, she genuinely shared similar interests to the prince. Charles proposed to Amanda in 1980 and The Queen is said to have been keen on the pairing, but Amanda turned the proposal down, citing the glare of the royal spotlight. Having trained as a social worker, Amanda married property entrepreneur Charles Ellingworth in October 1987. They have three sons.

Anna Wallace

The daughter of wealthy Scottish landowner Hamish Wallace, Charles began dating Anna - known within her circle as 'Whiplash Wallace' for her fiery attitude — in 1980. The Prince proposed twice but she turned him down both times. It was reported that Anna broke off their courtship during the Queen Mother's 80th birthday party after Charles had ignored her all evening, but it's also been suggested that the two parted ways due to the Prince's rekindled relationship with the married Camilla. '*Charles had taken her to two successive balls and then danced with Camilla for most of both evenings,*' royal author Penny Junor wrote. '*Anna dumped him with the words, "No one treats me like that — not even you".*' The couple had only just ended their relationship when Charles met Diana in the summer of 1980. Anna went on to marry twice — firstly entrepreneur, Johnny Hesketh, then city fund manager Tom Oates. Both marriages ended in divorce.

It was said Charles' recipe for the perfect woman involved her being '*aristocratic, tall, blonde, curvaceous, and with an English rose complexion.*' Lady Diana Spencer ticked all those boxes.

Right:
Anna Wallace, 31 January, 1980, who spent the weekend hunting with prince charles on the Cheshire hunt

Diana

'Whatever "in love" means'

Prince Charles' reply to journalists when asked if he was in love
with fiancée Lady Diana Spencer, February 1981

On paper, Lady Diana Spencer appeared to be the perfect bride for Prince Charles. At only 19-years-old when they became engaged, she was of aristocratic stock and there were no previous boyfriends to sully her reputation. She had never been in a proper relationship. However, the pairing proved to be one of the most ill-fated in recent Royal history.

Diana Frances Spencer, was born on July 1, 1961, at Park House near Sandringham, Norfolk. She was the youngest daughter of the then Viscount and Viscountess Althorp, now the late Earl Spencer and the late Honourable Mrs Shand-Kydd. Diana had two elder sisters, Jane and Sarah, and a younger brother, Charles. Her family lived on the Queen's estate at Sandringham where her father had rented Park House. He had been a royal equerry for both King George VI and the young Queen Elizabeth II. The Queen had been the chief guest when Diana's parents were married in 1954 - the ceremony at Westminster Abbey was one of the social events of the year.

When she was only six, Diana's parents split up. She would always remember the crunch of her mother's departing footsteps on the gravel drive. The children became pawns in a

Below Left:

Images from the Spencer family album

Right:

Image of Diana, released for official
Engagement

bitter custody dispute with her father eventually
winning main custody of Diana and her siblings, her
maternal grandmother Ruth Fermoy having given
evidence against her own daughter, Frances.

Lady Diana was sent to boarding school, eventually
attending West Heath Public School in Kent. Here she
excelled at sport, particularly swimming, but she failed all
her O levels. Nevertheless, in later years she recalled fond
school day memories, and supported her old school. She
spent a short time at finishing school in Switzerland before
moving to London, having persuaded her father to buy her a flat.
She worked first as a nanny, occasionally a cook, and then as an
assistant at the 'Young England' kindergarten in Knightsbridge.

Though she first met Prince Charles at the age of 16, Diana
knew many people in his family - Queen Elizabeth II was her
brother's godmother, and she played with Charles's brothers
as a child. In November 1977, Prince Charles met Lady Diana
for the first time at Althorp House, her 1,500-acre family estate
in Northamptonshire, England. At the time, he was dating
her older sister, Sarah, and had travelled up to join her for a
shooting weekend. In a later interview, he'd recall of this initial
meeting, *'how jolly and what fun she (Diana) was'*. In February
1978, Charles and Sarah went on a ski weekend to Klosters in

Switzerland. It is here that she is said to have told a journalist that she wouldn't marry anyone '*if he were the dustman or the King of England if she didn't love him.*' It's believed Charles ended their relationship soon afterwards. However, both Spencer sisters remained in his circle, even attending his 30th birthday party in November 1978 at Buckingham Palace.

It was 18 months later when Charles and Diana met again. Both were staying at a mutual friend's country house for the weekend. There, Diana emphatically talked to Charles about the recent death of his beloved great-uncle, Lord Mountbatten.

'*The next minute, he leapt on me, practically,*' she said according to the documentary 'Diana in her Own Words'. '*But then it sort of built up from there.*'

In September 1980, paparazzi cameras captured Diana at Balmoral and the secret of their relationship became public knowledge. Only five months later, Charles proposed to Diana at Windsor Castle. She accepted although it's thought the couple had only gone out

Below:

Althorp House

Right:

Lady Diana Spencer reveals her sapphire and diamond engagement ring while she and Prince Charles pose for photographs in the grounds of Buckingham Palace following the announcement of their engagement

a dozen or so times. The press attention reached fever pitch with Diana once bursting into tears at the wheel of her car.

'*I know it's just a job they have to do, but sometimes I do wish they wouldn't,*' she said of the photographers.

The engagement also saw her moving from the flat she shared with three friends to Clarence House, the home of the Queen Mother. The Royal betrothal was formally announced to the world on February 24 1981. When a reporter asks Charles if they were

in love, he famously — and fatefully - replied, *'Whatever "in love" means'*. Less than a month after the engagement, Prince Charles flew to Australia and New Zealand for five weeks, leaving his new fiancée behind. Diana was spotted crying at Heathrow airport upon his departure–but not because she was sad. It was much later revealed that just before he left, Charles had taken a phone call with married lover, Camilla Parker-Bowles.

'It just broke my heart,' Diana later recalled.

July 29 1981. . . the Royal wedding day at St Paul's Cathedral in London. Diana expressed doubts before walking down the aisle– especially after, it's said, she found a bracelet which Charles had

had made for Camilla. Her sisters, Jane and Sarah, told her it was too late to call it off, what with her name already being on the tea towels. So, Diana went ahead with the wedding, wearing a fairy tale gown in ivory satin designed by David and Elizabeth Emanuel, and the Spencer tiara. An estimated 750 million people around the globe watched the wedding.

The marriage was in trouble practically as soon as it had begun. On the first part of their honeymoon, cruising around the Mediterranean on the Royal Yacht Britannia, their lack of common interests formed an immediate gulf — as did the 12-year difference in their ages. The second part at Balmoral was even worse. Despite having claimed to adore country pursuits, it was clear Diana was actually a city girl. The fact that she was newly pregnant and suffering from morning sickness hardly helped matters. A few months later on into her pregnancy, it is said she threw herself down the stairs at Balmoral in a cry for help. In June 1982, Diana gave birth to her first child, Prince William. Afterwards, she suffered from postnatal depression.

'You'd wake up in the morning feeling you didn't want to get out of bed, you felt misunderstood, and just very, very low in yourself,' she was to say in 1995.

Above:

Lady Diana Spencer, wearing an Emanuel wedding dress, prepares to enter St. Paul's Cathedral on the arm of her father, Earl Spencer, for her wedding to Prince Charles, Prince of Wales

Right:

Leaving St Paul's Cathedral, as The Prince & Princess Of Wales

Below:

Press photographers and crowds of wellwishers outside Buckingham
Palace on the day of Prince Charles wedding to Lady Diana Spencer

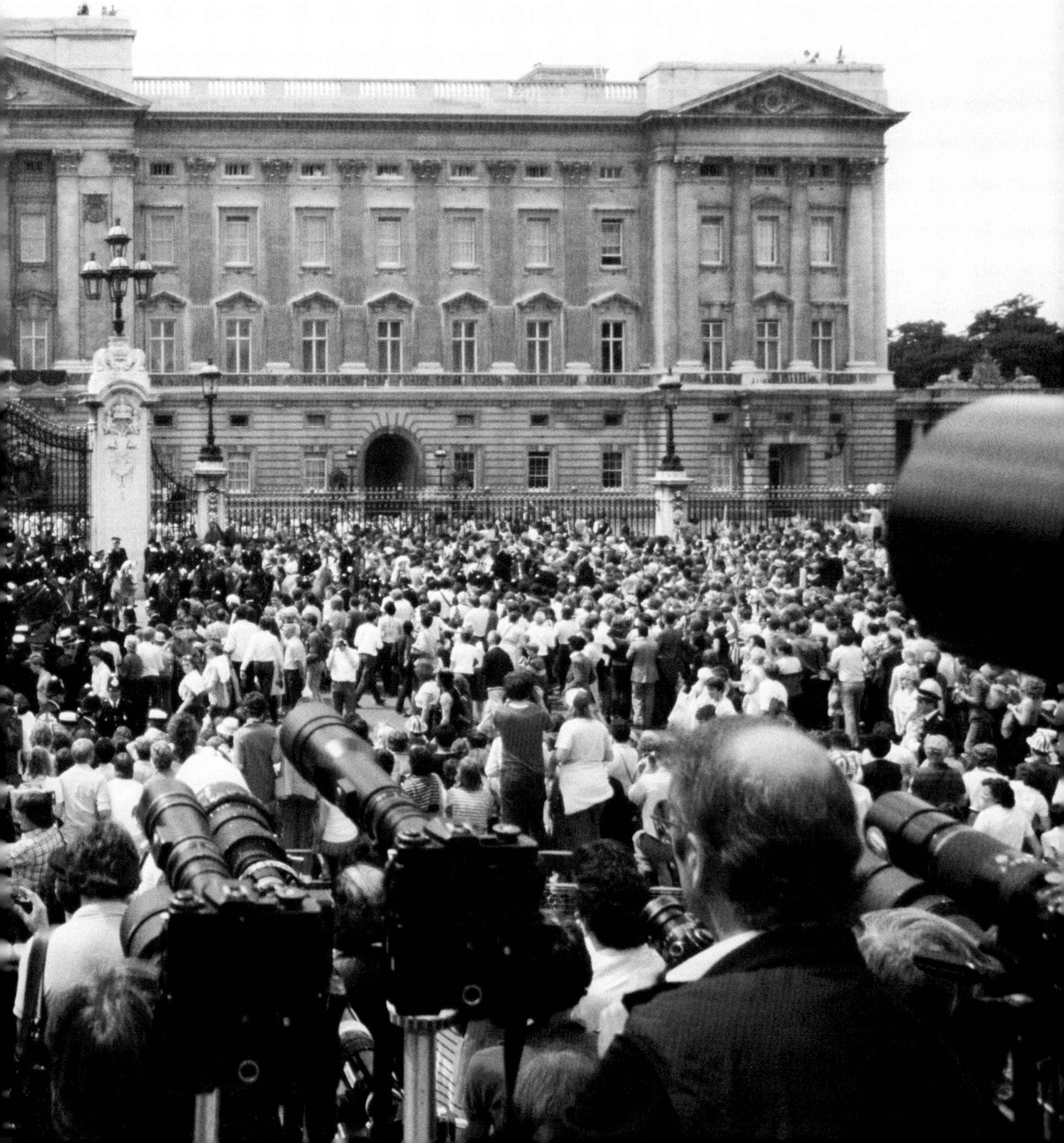

Above:

Diana Princess of Wales and Prince Charles with new
born Prince Harry, leave St Mary's on September 16 1984

The joy in being new parents marked a few, relatively happy and peaceful years for the couple. In September 1984, second son Prince Harry was born, but the marriage was already on life support. Apart from their sons, there was no common ground between the couple, plus Charles was said to be jealous of the adoration the public felt for his young wife. They were desperately unhappy and by 1986, Charles had resumed his affair with Camilla. It's thought that Diana's affair with army Captain James Hewitt started at around the same time.

'How awful incompatibility is, and how dreadfully destructive it can be for the players in this extraordinary drama,' Charles wrote to an unidentified correspondent. *'It has all the ingredients of a Greek tragedy.'*

The next few years saw Charles and Diana plagued with rumours of marital strife. In 1987, Diana failed to join Charles on the family's annual summer trip to Balmoral, leading press headlines to speculate on a *'Royal break'*. During several public appearances, they seemed distant and unhappy with each other.

'Diana was the love object of everyone in the world except her husband. She was faced in her mid-twenties with something she found chilling to contemplate - a fairy-tale marriage that had cooled into an arrangement,' wrote a Vanity Fair journalist.

In May 1992, Andrew Morton published 'Diana: Her True Story', a blistering tell-all of the collapse of the Wales' marriage, Charles's affair with Camilla Parker Bowles, and Diana's own mental health struggles. Secretly, the princess had cooperated with the book, providing Morton with audio recordings. In November of that year, Charles and Diana went on an official trip to South Korea together. They looked so miserable that the British press referred to them as *'the Glums'*. Just one month later, British Prime Minister John Major announced to the House of Commons that the Prince and Princess of Wales were separating.

'This decision has been reached amicably and they will both continue to participate fully in the upbringing of their children,' he read from a Buckingham Palace Statement.

Neither Charles nor Diana commented. Instead, Charles attended a business luncheon and Diana visited a clinic in northeast England. The palace told reporters that no third party was involved in the decision, all despite tabloid reports and Morton's book.

The drama threw the monarchy into deep turmoil.

'The news of the separation comes at a time when the credibility of the monarchy is at a modern low-point as a result of persistent reports alluding to the marital scandals and wealthy lifestyle of some members of the Royal family,' commented one broadsheet newspaper at the time.

Diana said that she felt *'deep, deep, profound sadness'* about their decision, adding that. *'We had struggled to keep it going, but obviously we'd both run out of steam.'* She also famously alluded to Camilla Parker Bowles by saying, *'There were three of us in the marriage so it was a bit crowded'.*

After coming to an agreement in July 1996, Prince Charles and Princess Diana's divorce was finalised that August. Diana received a significant financial settlement, but was stripped of her 'Her Royal Highness' status. Tragically, her new, liberated post-royal life was cut short after a fatal car crash in Paris a year later.

According to Royal expert, Christopher Andersen, Prince Charles was left *'ashen and trembling with the phone in his hand'* as he learnt of Diana's death.

'He then let out a cry of pain that was so spontaneous and came from the heart,' Andersen further shared, also citing one witness describing it as a *'howl of anguish'*. *'Staff rushed over to Charles' room and found him collapsed in an armchair, weeping uncontrollably. I don't think people realize how really stricken he was by her death. I interviewed the nurses in the hospital who saw him when he came into the room and saw her body for the first time. And he looked like he'd been hit in the face. He reeled back. They thought he was going to faint. They were surprised to see how emotional Charles was after her death.'*

Left:

Prince William & Diana pose for portraits in the sitting room of their home in Kensington Palace

Right:

Prince Charles, Prince of Wales, with his sons Princes William and Harry looking at floral tributes left at Kensington Palace following the death of Diana, Princess of Wales in September, 1997

Camilla

'My great-grandmother was the mistress of your great-great-grandfather I feel we have something in common'

Camilla Shand to Prince Charles on their first meeting in 1971

Camilla Parker-Bowles and Prince Charles are thought to have resumed their relationship as lovers in late 1978 or early 1979. By then she had two children with husband, Andrew — Tom born in late 1974 and Laura born in early 1978. It was common knowledge within their social circle that Andrew had been unfaithful to Camilla throughout their marriage and, although she put a brave face on it, deep down she felt hurt and unloved. There was absolutely no question of Camilla divorcing her husband and marrying Charles. They were best friends and lovers — and that was surely all they ever could be. It was unthinkable at the time to think that they would eventually marry. After he had proposed to Diana in early 1981, Charles knew that his intimate relationship with Camilla had to end. Whether Camilla did or not is open to debate. Certainly Diana, although young and naïve, knew instinctively that her husband-to-be's relationship with Camilla was not platonic. Mrs Parker Bowles took Diana out for a girly lunch during which, Diana was to say in retrospect, Camilla questioned her about whether she intended to hunt to hounds and spend much time at Highgrove — Charles' newly-acquired country home in Gloucestershire - after the marriage. Diana also couldn't understand why Camilla seemed to know so much.

'She (Camilla) kept saying to me, "Don't push him into doing this, don't do that",' Diana was later to say. *'She knew so much about what he was doing privately and what we were doing privately. I couldn't understand it. Eventually I worked it all out.'*

An intuitive woman, Camilla realised that Diana had a problem with her and purposely began to distance herself from Charles. However, they still spoke regularly on the phone. Charles wanted

Left:

Prince Charles and Camilla Parker-Bowles are seen together in late 1979 before his marriage to Diana

Right:

Camilla, then, Duchess of Cornwall at Epsom Down's Racecourse to officially open the new Duchess Stand

six-year-old Tom Parker Bowles, his godson, to be one of the page boys at the Royal Wedding but Diana vetoed the idea. There were many blazing rows between Charles and Diana during their five-month engagement — mostly over Camilla. However, Charles vowed to Diana that since their engagement there had been no other women in his life, there would be no others and he expected Diana to believe him.

Camilla attended the Royal Wedding with her sister, Annabel. But there was no invite to the reception at Buckingham Palace — at Diana's insistence. Camilla had lost her lover and confidante while husband Andrew, who had been on duty with the Household Cavalry at the wedding, had begun yet another passionate affair — this time with Charlotte Hambro, mother of bridesmaid, Clementine. Over the next few years, Camilla must have heard through the grapevine that Charles and Diana's marriage wasn't a success but apart from sending Christmas cards and seeing Charles from afar at occasional hunt meets, Camilla kept her distance and her own counsel. But by 1986, mutual friends of Charles and Camilla contacted her because they were worried about the Prince. He was moody, withdrawn, morose and generally very difficult. They asked her to phone him — the thought being that only Camilla would be able to cheer him up. Eventually she called.

At first there were just phone conversations but then Charles started inviting Camilla to Highgrove when Diana wasn't there — usually in the company of friends. By now the Prince and Princess of Wales could hardly bear to be in the same room together. The love affair between Charles and Camilla resumed with Charles visiting Camilla at home when Andrew and the children were away, and Camilla going to Highgrove when neither Diana nor their sons were in residence. They also met at the houses of supportive friends. Charles later admitted to being unfaithful to Diana but said it was only after his marriage had *irretrievably broken down, us both having tried'.*

Above:

Andrew and Camilla-Parker Bowles attend the Queen's Cup polo match at Windsor, 7th June 1992

Left:

Camilla Parker-Bowles on horseback during a hunt in Wiltshire, in 1995 in which Prince Charles also participated

Charles and Camilla's affair stayed secret until the early 1990s, although Diana was certainly aware soon after it started up again. In 1989, Diana decided to confront her husband's lover at a party. If it was Diana's aim to split Charles and Camilla as a result, it didn't succeed. Diana was also conducting a love affair with James Hewitt at this time.

The years 1992 and 1993 changed everything for Diana, Charles and Camilla. The Prince and Mrs Parker-Bowles' affair became public knowledge after the publication of Andrew Morton's book 'Diana: Her True Story' in 1992. Both Charles and Camilla were vilified in the press. While the Prince was, to a certain extent, used to this, the same could not be said of Camilla. She was suddenly a scarlet woman who was seen to be damaging Charles and Diana's marriage. The paparazzi had her under siege and she couldn't leave home without being jostled and photographed. Then, poison pen letters started to arrive. Media pressure focused more on Diana when 'Squidgygate' came to light. This was the nickname for the recording of an intimate 1989 phone-call between Diana and supposed lover, James Gilbey — the transcript of which was printed in a British tabloid. Diana was said to be deeply embarrassed and at the end of 1992 — Queen Elizabeth II's 'Annus Horribilis' — it was announced that the Prince and Princess of Wales were separating but that no third parties were involved. It was hoped the dust would settle somewhat after the announcement but then, less than a month into 1993, 'Camillagate' emerged. This was the recording of a deeply intimate conversation between Charles and Camilla, the transcription of which was published in a British tabloid with the truly gobsmacking revelation the future king had idly mused about being his beloved Camilla's tampon. The tapes caused a huge scandal for the Royal Family and seemingly confirmed the persistent rumours of affairs on both sides. In 1994, Charles finally spoke about his relationship with Camilla in the TV documentary 'Charles: The Private Man, the Public Role' and admitted that Mrs Parker-Bowles was his lover. Once again, Camilla had to run the gauntlet of the tabloid press.

Andrew Parker-Bowles had been perfectly accommodating about his wife's affair with Prince Charles since it had started up again in 1986 — until, that is, it was on the front page of every newspaper. He felt his hand had been forced and Charles' confession had completely undermined his position. Camilla was shocked when Andrew told her he wanted a divorce but his mind was made up. He had realised that Camilla was genuinely in love with Charles plus his own paramour, Rose Pitman, was recently divorced and free to marry. It would be a relatively straightforward divorce — mainly because it was so amicable. In December 1994, Andrew and Camilla jointly filed for divorce on the grounds that they had been living apart for two years. However, Camilla felt very vulnerable afterwards. She no longer had the protection of her marriage, the family home was sold plus her mother had recently passed away. Her future was uncertain, she was still being hounded and vilified by the press — likewise by members of her family. She found a house of her own in Wiltshire, 'Ray Mill', and life started to calm down a little but then, in late 1995, Diana recorded her explosive interview with the BBC's Panorama programme. Queen Elizabeth II finally lost her patience and insisted that Charles and Diana divorce. Their decree absolute was finalised in July 1996.

Camilla had no ambitions to become a public figure — or indeed Charles' second wife. She envisaged seeing him whenever his busy schedule allowed and being free to take holidays and spend weekends together. However, she tentatively started to do some high-profile work for charity and gradually, her image as Royal mistress/scarlet woman began to change.

Right:
Prince Charles, the Prince of Wales and Camilla Parker-Bowles leave the Royal Festival Hall after the performance Of Rachmaninoff's Hidden Perspectives on May 6th, 1999 in London

'A new chapter has opened up in the life of Camilla Parker-Bowles,' wrote the Daily Mirror, to accompany formal photographs that had been taken of her in early 1997. *'This is the picture that proves it. Now she is rid of the role of furtive mistress, she can look into the camera with confidence and without fear. Most people found it difficult to see why Prince Charles would divorce stunning Diana to spend time with Camilla but now we can see for ourselves a little bit of the magic he fell in love with.'*

Charles was said to be on the verge of formally introducing Camilla to the public as his partner when Diana was tragically killed. After Diana's death, Camilla deliberately went to ground, realising that Charles needed to concentrate on his sons. She also knew that it would be months before they would be able to be seen in public together. They continued to speak at least once a day and met whenever possible. Then in July 1998, royal aides confirmed that Camilla had met Prince William and would meet Prince Harry at a later date. That same year, Charles celebrated his 50th birthday with a large party at Highgrove arranged by Camilla — although Queen Elizabeth II declined the invitation. As far as Charles was concerned, Camilla's role in his life was non-negotiable and in 1999, the couple slowly began attending events together. Charles threw a 50th birthday party for Camilla's sister at the Ritz Hotel in January 1999, where Charles and Camilla were photographed together for the first time. Although

they arrived at the party separately, they left together in full view of reporters and photographers. The next year — millennium year -Queen Elizabeth II met Camilla for the first time in years when both attended a 60th birthday celebration for the King of Greece at Highgrove. It was seen as the Queen's seal of approval. It was also in 2000 that Camilla accompanied Charles to Scotland for a number of official engagements and then in 2001, she became president of the Royal Osteoporosis Society (ROS), which introduced her to the public.

Left:

Prince Charles, the Prince of Wales, and Camilla the Duchess of Cornwall, leave St George's Chapel, Windsor, following the blessing of their wedding

Right:

Prince Charles, the Prince of Wales, and the Duchess of Cornwall, Camilla Parker-Bowles, inside St George's Chapel in Windsor Castle for the Service of Prayer and Dedication for their marriage blessing

After a series of appearances at public and private venues, the Queen invited Camilla to her Golden Jubilee celebrations in 2002. She sat in the royal box behind the Queen for one of the concerts at Buckingham Palace. Charles also started to pay privately for two full-time security staff for her protection. Although Camilla maintained her 'Ray Mill House', she moved into Clarence House, Charles' official residence since 2003 which he inherited following the death of his beloved grandmother, Queen Elizabeth the Queen Mother, in 2002. In 2004, Camilla accompanied Charles on almost all of his official events, including a high-profile visit together to the annual highland games in Scotland. On 10 February 2005, Clarence House announced that Mrs Parker-Bowles and the Prince of Wales were engaged. As an engagement ring, Charles gave Camilla a diamond ring believed to have been given to his grandmother, Queen Elizabeth the Queen Mother, when she gave birth to Charles' mother. As the future supreme governor of the Church of England, the prospect of Charles marrying a divorcée was seen as controversial, but with the consent of the Queen, the government, and the Church of England, the couple were able to wed. The Queen, Prime Minister Tony Blair and Archbishop of Canterbury Rowan Williams offered their best wishes in statements to the media.

The marriage was to have been a civil ceremony at Windsor Castle, with a subsequent religious service of blessing at St George's Chapel. However, to conduct a civil marriage at Windsor Castle would oblige the venue to obtain a licence for civil marriages, which it did not have, plus a condition of such a licence is that the licensed venue must be available for a period

Left:

Prince Charles, The Prince of Wales and The Duchess Of Cornwall, Camilla Parker-Bowles pose for the Official Wedding photograph with their children and parents (L-R Prince Harry, Prince William, Laura and Tom Parker-Bowles Front: Queen Elizabeth II, Prince Philip, Bruce Shand), in the White Drawing Room at Windsor Castle following their marriage. Saturday April 9 2005, in Windsor

of one year to anyone wishing to be married there. As the Royal Family did not wish to make Windsor Castle available to the public for civil marriages, the venue was changed to the town hall at Windsor Guildhall. On 4 April, it was announced that the marriage would be delayed by one day to allow the Prince of Wales to attend thefuneral of Pope John Paul II.

On 9 April 2005, the marriage ceremony was held. The parents of Charles and Camilla did not attend. Instead, Camilla's son Tom and Charles's son Prince William acted as witnesses to the union. The Queen and the Duke of Edinburgh did, however attend the service of blessing. Afterwards, a reception was held by the Queen for the newlyweds at Windsor Castle.

'They have overcome Becher's Brook and the Chair and all kinds of other terrible obstacles,' she said, referring to the notoriously challenging Aintree Racecourse at the annual Grand National steeplechase. *'They have come through and I'm very proud and wish them well. My son is home and dry with the woman he loves.'*

Following the wedding, the couple travelled to Birkhall, the Prince's country home in Scotland, and carried out their first public duties together during their honeymoon. Although officially entitled to use title 'The Princess of Wales', Camilla let it be

known she would be addressed as 'The Duchess of Cornwall'.

In 2015, the couple celebrated their 15th wedding anniversary. That same year, during an interview with CNN, Charles talked about his relationship with his beloved second wife.

'It's always marvellous to have somebody who, you know, you feel understands and wants to encourage,' he said. 'Although she certainly pokes fun if I get too serious about things. And all that helps."

Left:

Camilla with Charles and Queen Elizabeth II in a carriage, 2012

Above:

The Duchess Of Cornwall at Barn Croft Primary School for a Commonwealth Big Lunch event, 2018. Camilla has been the initiative's patron since 2013

In February 2022, Queen Elizabeth II announced it was her wish that Camilla become Queen once Charles ascended the throne.

'When, in the fullness of time, my son Charles becomes King, I know you will give him and his wife Camilla the same support that you have given me, and it is my sincere wish that, when that time comes, Camilla will be known as Queen Consort as she continues her own loyal service,' Queen Elizabeth wrote in a message shared on the eve of her Accession Day.

On September 8, 2022, the Royal Family confirmed the passing of Queen Elizabeth II. Charles and Camilla immediately assumed the roles of King and Queen Consort.

'I count on the loving help of my darling wife, Camilla,' said Charles in his first speech as King Charles III. *'In recognition of her own loyal public service since our marriage 17 years ago, she becomes my Queen Consort. I know she will bring to the demands of her new role the steadfast devotion to duty on which I have come to rely so much.'*

Family Matters

*'Relationships with fathers can be such complex ones....
So often, I suppose, one must long to have got on better or to have been
able to talk freely about the things that matter deeply but one was too
inhibited to discuss'*

King Charles III, when Prince of Wales, on father-son relationships

I t became obvious early on that, as a young boy, the often dreamy and always sensitive Prince Charles had little in common with his straightforward, undemonstrative parents. Indeed, when Charles' cousin, Lady Pamela was asked which parent Charles was most like, she quipped, *'I think he must be a changeling.'*

As was the case with many upper-class parents of time, the then Princess Elizabeth and the Duke of Edinburgh weren't exactly 'hands-on' with their offspring. This was exacerbated when the Princess became Queen when Charles was only three-years-old.

'I think any idea of a family in the normal sense was knocked on the head by the queen's accession at such an early age,' commented royal writer Philip Ziegler.

Eizabeth II was now facing overwhelming responsibilities and a never-ending schedule of royal activities. Charles recalled

Left:
Princess Elizabeth and Prince Philip, Duke of Edinburgh at Buckingham Palace shortly before their wedding

Right:
Princess Elizabeth and the Duke of Edinburgh on honeymoon at Broadlands in Hampshire

her entering the bathroom while his nanny was giving him his evening bath.

'Mummy was a remote and glamorous figure who came to kiss you goodnight, smelling of lavender and dressed for dinner,' Charles recalled.

Elizabeth and Philip undoubtedly loved Charles and his younger sister, Anne, but it was very much parenting from a distance. In 1953, the newly crowned Elizabeth and Prince Philip went on a six-month tour of the commonwealth, leaving Charles and Anne in the UK. According to reports, Elizabeth cried as she left her children but their reunion after half a year away was hardly loving. Charles raced on board the royal yacht Britannia to welcome his mother and father home. He ran up to join the group of dignitaries waiting to shake her hand. When the Queen saw

Left:

Princess Elizabeth with her baby son Prince Charles

Below:

The two youngest children of Queen Elizabeth, Prince Andrew, left, and baby, Prince Edward

her young son squirming in line, she said, *'No, not you, dear.'* She did not hug him or kiss him. She simply patted his shoulder and passed along to the next person.

It was Charles' beloved nanny, Mabel Anderson, who gave the young prince the tactile love and affection he so craved.

'For Prince Charles, who had already discovered that only in

the nursery could he always be assured of a cuddle, Mabel Anderson became "a haven of security, the great haven" to whom he invariably turned first for comfort and support,' Jonathan Dimbleby wrote in his 1994 book, 'The Prince of Wales: A Biography' with which Charles cooperated.

In his grandmother Queen Elizabeth, the Queen Mother, the first in a long line of older matriarchs the prince would become close with, Charles found a kindred spirit who would nurture his love of arts and culture. The Queen Mother also advocated on Charles's behalf against his formidable father. The Queen, overburdened with duties, let her husband make most decisions regarding their children and Philip often bullied his son in an attempt to toughen him up.

'Observing friends were also frustrated by the failure of the child's mother to intervene by protective word or gesture,' Dimbleby wrote. 'She was not indifferent so much as detached, deciding that in domestic matters she would submit entirely to the father's will.'

Princess Anne wasn't troubled by this but then she was very much her father's daughter. Charles had different needs which

Above:

Queen Elizabeth, the Queen Mother (1900-2002) sits with her grandchildren Prince Charles, Princess Anne and baby Prince Andrew, August 1960

Left:

Elizabeth II with her son Prince Andrew in a pram and Princess Anne, September 1960

his parents seemed unable to meet. As young Charles grew into adulthood, formality was the norm. He would be forced to schedule meetings if he wanted to see his parents and only learnt of what they were doing by reading a schedule sent around every day. It undoubtedly caused him pain to see how differently his mother parented her two younger sons, Andrew and Edward, both of whom were born in the 1960s when Elizabeth had settled into her role and had more time. Charles continued to lean on his grandmother while also seeking out surrogate maternal figures, like Deborah Cavendish, Duchess of Devonshire.

Above:

New born Prince Andrew in Queen Elizabeth II's arms, March, 1960

Left:

Queen Elizabeth II and Prince Philip, Duke of Edinburgh and their children at Windsor on the Queen's 39th birthday, April 1965

He also turned to his great uncle Louis Mountbatten for advice and emotional support.

'Charles was unable to turn to his parents to discuss the misery either of his private life or of his public persona,' writes Dimbleby. *'Their response to his charitable endeavours was incurious, while he was rarely left in doubt that they did not entirely welcome his contributions to controversial debate. The emotional gulf between the Prince and his parents was hard to bridge, while communication between them was normally limited to the exchange of social pleasantries and the formal business of the family enterprise.'*

There was also the natural tension between mother and son over the delicate fact that until the queen's abdication or death, her son would forever be in limbo. However, when Charles chose to air his grievances to Jonathan Dimbleby in 1994, his parents and siblings were hurt with Princess Anne saying the insinuation her parents were not caring was *'just beggar's belief'*.

However, as the years passed, the Queen began to recognize Charles's enormous charitable contributions. Plus, once he had married Camilla, the mother-son relationship greatly improved. Mother and son shared several interests, including a love of the country, excellent comic timing, and a similar sense of the ridiculous.

In 2016, Prince Charles helped spearhead the documentary 'Elizabeth at 90: A Family Tribute'. The most touching scenes showed Charles and his 'mummy' sitting side by side watching footage from family home movies. They chuckled and chatted, and the warmth of their relationship was unmistakable. The Queen also shared dispatch contents with her son and heir, and deferred increasingly to him as he essentially operated as a 'shadow king' in the time before her death. At Charles' 70th birthday party in November 2018, the speech she gave demonstrated how much she loved him.

'I have seen Charles become a champion of conservation and the arts, a great charitable leader–a dedicated and respected heir to the throne to stand comparison with any in history–and a wonderful father,' she said. *'Most of all, sustained by his wife, Camilla, he is his own man, passionate and creative. So, this toast is to wish a happy birthday to my son, in every respect a duchy original.'*

As a father himself, Charles was often absent. During their early childhood, there were many photos of both William and Harry with their mother, Diana, on royal tours and at charitable visits but rarely any images of just Charles and his young sons.

'When we were kids, there were bags and bags and bags of work that the office just sent to him,' Harry said in the 2018 BBC One documentary, 'Prince, Son and Heir: Charles at 70'. *'We could barely even get to his desk to say goodnight to him.'*

It's true to say that the Prince was more remote figure than 'dad' when the boys were young.

Left:

Princess Diana cuddling her baby son, Prince Harry, aboard the Royal Yacht Britannia during her tour of Italy in May 1985

Right:

Prince William giggles with his hand over his mouth as he and baby brother, Harry, pretended to play the piano during a private photo session at home in Kensington Palace, October 1985

'It was a slightly tricky relationship because Charles has always been quite remote, he has always been consumed by work,' Royal author and commentator Penny Junor told the 'Daily Beast'. 'That's not a product of a lack of love. It's a product of the fact he is so focused on his work, and the need to make a difference in the world that, like many people who are seeking to make a difference in the world, he has sometimes overlooked friends and loved ones beside him.'

According to Prince Harry, it was after the death of their mother in 1997 that his and William's relationship with Charles grew stronger.

'One of the hardest things for a parent to have to do is to tell your children that your other parent has died,' Harry said in the 2017 BBC documentary 'Diana, 7 Days.' 'How you deal with that,

I don't know. He was there for us. He was the one out of two left, and he tried to do his best and to make sure that we were protected and looked after. But he was going through the same grieving process as well.'

Below:

Surrounded by Royal relatives and godparents who are amused at the antics of young Prince William, Prince Harry is christened at Windsor Castle on December 21, 1984

Right:

Prince Charles laughing with his sons as he lifts Prince Harry onto Prince William's shoulders in Kensington Palace

After Diana's death, Prince Charles understood he needed to respect his sons' feelings, so he made sure that it was the two of them who dictated when they met his partner, Camilla.

'Charles was always sensitive about William and Harry's feelings regarding Camilla,' Penny Junor wrote in 'The Daily Telegraph'. *'It was never going to be easy but the boys dictated the pace and soon realised that Camilla made their father enormously happy, and that his happiness was more important than anything else.'*

Charles has always played two roles in his sons' lives. He's their father but also their boss — although this ceased to be the case with Harry when he stepped back from Royal duties in 2020. Over the years, there has been tension between father and sons regarding money.

'There has always been this complicated relationship with their dad,' a source told People magazine before Harry left the 'firm'. *'It's not a straightforward father-son relationship. He is their father and their boss, and they are beholden to him to fund their offices and lives. Tension between Charles and the boys has always surrounded money, because Charles is the one who holds all the power.'*

According to reports, since William became a husband and father, he and his father have grown closer.

'Since becoming a father I think William and his father are very much on the same page,' a source has said. *'There's a sense of duty that runs through them both and unites them and as far as*

Left:

Catherine, Duchess of Cambridge, Princess Charlotte of Cambridge and Prince George of Cambridge, Prince William, Duke of Cambridge at a children's party for Military families during the Royal Tour of Canada on September 29, 2016 in Victoria, Canada

their relationship is concerned, they've crossed a bridge. As both Charles and William are in line for the throne, they understand each other. They are on the same wavelength these days and when Charles talks about William it is with great pride. You often hear him talk of sovereignty and how they bond over this commitment to sovereignty. They will both be kings one day - and William's oldest son will be king - and that is something that connects them and has brought them closer in recent years.'

While William's relationship with his father has become closer in recent years, Harry's has suffered. In Harry and Meghan Markle's tell-all interview with Oprah Winfrey in 2022 and then also in the Netflix documentary, 'Harry and Meghan', Harry revealed that his father cut him off completely. A spokesperson for Charles revealed that he had actually paid for Harry and his wife until the summer of 2020, insisting that their exit had been *'a matter of enormous sadness to the family'* and that nobody had wanted to suddenly abandon the couple.

'But Charles wanted to help make this work, and allocated a substantial sum to the Duke and Duchess of Sussex, to help them with that transition,' the spokesman continued. An inside source also gave Vanity Fair the future King's side of the story, claiming, *'Charles was quite upset at the suggestion he had cut Harry off.'*

Despite initially continuing to pay for his son, apparently *'there was a point when Charles decided enough was enough'* and called off their finances. *'The bank of dad couldn't keep handing out indefinitely,'* the source added.

At the time of writing, it's thought that father and younger son remain estranged with King Charles only seeing his grandchildren, Archie and Lilibet, on a handful of occasions.

'There's a lot to work through,' Harry told Oprah. *'I feel really let down because he's been through something similar. He knows what pain is like. Of course, I will always love him, but there's a lot of hurt that's happened.'*

Charles may barely know Archie and Lilibet Mountbatten-Windsor, however his relationship with Prince George, Princess Charlotte and Prince Louis of Wales mirrors the close relationship he had with his own maternal grandmother, the Queen Mother. Charles never really knew his grandpa – Queen Elizabeth's father, King George VI, died in 1952 when the prince was just a toddler – but the strong connection he had with his grandmother left a lasting impression on him. Knowing how special the bond between grandparents and grandchildren can be, Charles has shown a strong desire to have a loving relationship with the young royals – particularly George, who is third-in-line to the throne. Being a grandparent has been deeply rewarding for Charles, whose life was largely consumed by royal duties when his own sons were growing up.

'Being a grandparent is a different part of your life,' he said in 2013, according to 'The Daily Telegraph'. *'The great thing is to encourage grandchildren. Show them things to take their interest. My grandmother did that, she was wonderful. It is very important to create a bond when they are very young.'*

Unfortunately, it looks very much like Charles will be unable to create such a bond with Harry's children.

Below:

Prince Louis of Cambridge sits on his grandfather Prince Charles, Prince of Wales's lap as they attend the Platinum Pageant on The Mall on June 5, 2022 in London

Right:

Prince Harry and actress Meghan Markle during an official photocall to announce their engagement

Philanthropy, Passions, Projects and Pastimes

'I find myself born into this particular position I'm determined to make the most of it and to do whatever I can to help. And I hope I leave things behind a little better than I found them All the time I feel I must justify my existence'

King Charles III

For over 40 years, Charles has been a leader in identifying philanthropic need, then driving forward charities to meet it. Together with Camilla, he is president or patron of more than 500 organisations. Charles is also the president of 19 charitable trusts. These trusts raise over £100 million annually for their chosen causes, all of which are overseen by Charles himself. His charities also have branches in Canada and Australia which help him further his philanthropic endeavours around the globe. As Prince of Wales, Charles frequently toured both nations, attending charitable events in an effort to bring aid to youth, the disabled, the disadvantaged, the arts, the environment and so many more causes.

Charles started his charity 'The Prince's Trust' with his Navy severance pay of just over £7,000 back in 1976. To date, the Trust has helped over 875,000 disadvantaged young people into employment or business.

'Over the last 40 years, the work of my Trust has shown it is within our power to transform young lives for the better,' he said on the Trust's 40th anniversary in 2016.

Charles has also founded a number of initiatives to try and help communities, locally and globally, across the world. Many of these focus on his passion for sustainability. One of these is

'The Prince's Accounting for Sustainability Project', founded in 2004, which aims to inspire action by finance leaders to drive a fundamental shift toward resilient business models and a sustainable economy. Another is the campaign for wool, where Charles sought to repopularise wool as a natural fire-retardant and sustainable fabric, expanding the market for both British and Commonwealth wool as well as promoting the awareness of its environmental benefits. He also set up the Prince's Countryside Fund (PCF), helping to improve the quality of life for those living and working in rural areas. The PCF has a vision of a confident, robust and sustainable agricultural and rural community which is universally appreciated for its vital contribution to the British way of life and fits to support future generations.

As a passionate devotee of classical architecture, modernist buildings have been a frequent target of the King's ire over the years. A former Brutalist library in Birmingham was *a place where books are incinerated, not kept*, he once said.

Above:

The, Prince of Wales, President of The Prince's Trust meets staff and young people involved in the Launched in Lockdown Programme during a visit to The Prince's Trust, Cymru on July 9, 2021 in Cardiff

Prince Charles visiting a community centre
in Manchester in 1983 for the Prince's Trust
project and being shown work on a computer

On another occasion, a reading room for the British Library in
London struck him as resembling '*an assembly hall of an academy
for secret police*'. While on a boat tour on the Thames in 1988,
according to one biographer, the Prince pivoted from quoting
Wordsworth on the glory of Westminster Bridge to training his sights
on architect Denys Lasdun's Royal National Theatre, a 'Brutalist'
complex of buildings. The then HRH dismissed it as '*a clever way
of building a nuclear power station in the middle of London*'. Then
of course there is his famous 1984 comment likening the design to
the new extension on London's National Gallery to '*a monstrous
carbuncle on the face of a much-loved and elegant friend*'. At a
gala for planners, Charles once proclaimed, '*You have to give this
much to the Luftwaffe - when it knocked down our buildings, it didn't
replace them with anything more offensive than rubble.*'

Charles' opinions have led to certain building projects being
scrapped. The architect Richard Rogers, known for the Pompidou
Centre in Paris and Lloyd's Building in London, claimed that the
Prince of Wales jettisoned at least three of his projects. Another
project, a multibillion-pound development on the site of the former
Chelsea Barracks, was cancelled by Qatar's royal family after an
'*act of princely sabotage*', the architect alleged.

In the creation of Poundbury, the future King was able to witness
his ideal architectural vision realised. In 1989, he helped
launch the experimental community, an extension of the city of
Dorchester, constructed in accordance with Charles' theories on
design. The project, which is still unfolding, is due to be completed
in 2025, with some 1500 homes and nearly 200 businesses

arranged along terraced boulevards lined by columns and colonnades. Poundbury reflects four key principles: Architecture of place - creating beauty and reflecting local character and identity; Integrated affordable housing - throughout the development and indistinguishable from private housing; Mixed use - homes, public amenities, retail and other business uses together with open areas, all designed as an overall community; Walkable community - giving priority to people rather than to cars.

'*A merry riot of porticoes and pilasters, mansards and mouldings, sampling from the rich history of architectural pattern books with promiscuous glee,*' is how the Guardian newspaper colourfully described it.

As Poundbury has developed, it has demonstrated that there is a genuine alternative to the way in which new communities are built in the UK.

Below:

27 October 2017, in the Main Square of Poundbury, Prince Charles unveiled a statue in tribute to the late Queen Mother whose pedestal was designed by Léon Krier

Right:

Prince Charles meets the cleanup crews at the site of the Sea Empress pollution disaster, 29 February 1996

'When I set out on this venture, I was determined that Poundbury would break the mould of conventional housing development in this country, and create an attractive place for people to live, work and play,' Charles has said. 'Many people said that it could never succeed but I am happy to say that the sceptics were wrong and it is now a thriving urban settlement alongside Dorchester.'

Charles' passion for the environment and sustainability is well-known.

'On an increasingly crowded planet, humanity faces many threats but none is greater than climate change. It magnifies every hazard and tension of our existence,' he said in 2015.

For over 50 years, as Prince of Wales, he used his unique position to champion action for a sustainable future. In the context of global challenges that include the climate crisis, deforestation, and ocean pollution, Charles has promoted sustainability to ensure that the natural assets upon which we all depend - among other things soil, water, forests, a stable climate and fish stocks - endure for future generations. He believes that economic and social development will best succeed when it works in harmony, rather than in conflict, with nature.

'There is an amazing amount that can be done,' he said in 2022. 'It is a combined responsibility of all of us — the public sector, private sector and civil society.'

Over the decades, the former Prince of Wales has launched a number of sustainability initiatives aimed at delivering practical outcomes. As well as addressing environmental challenges, Charles promotes a more sustainable approach to planning and designing homes and communities in ways that enhance and add to the social, natural and built environment — the prime example being Poundbury. His sustainability work is based on the principle that environmental challenges in our increasingly interconnected world are best met by adopting integrated and holistic approaches to sustainability. Charles has used his position to help raise public awareness about challenges and solutions through his speeches, articles, books and films. He is also Patron of a wide range of organizations working for sustainability, offering support and encouragement for their work.

In September 2018, the Prince received a special Lifetime Achievement Award from GQ Magazine for Services to Philanthropy. In an interview for the publication to celebrate the award he discussed the importance of sustainable fashion.

Right:

Charles, Prince of Wales, who is Patron of the marine conservation charity Surfers Against Sewage, addresses attendees by video link at the pre-G7 Summit Sustainable Growth Conference organised by the Cornwall Chamber of Commerce on June 08, 2021 in Falmouth, England. The video conference featured leading speakers from the Cornish business and environment sectors who demonstrated how the county has taken a lead in understanding and delivering sustainable projects in agritech, education, health and energy

Below:

The Prince of Wales arrives in his Aston Martin DB6 Volante, which is powered by surplus wine, to visit the new Aston Martin Lagonda factory on February 21, 2020 in St Athan, Wales

'I have always believed that living on a finite planet means we have to recognize that this puts certain constraints and limits on our human ambition in order to maintain the viability of the planet,' he said.

As well as promoting sustainability through his work, Charles has personally taken many steps to live in a more sustainable way. Around half of his office and domestic energy use comes from renewable sources such as woodchip boilers, air-source heat pumps, solar panels and 'green' electricity. His households strive to minimise their environmental impact across their activities, including travel, energy use and the indirect impact of the products and services it uses. Famously, he had his Aston Martin DB6 re-engineered for alternative fuel and it runs on a combination of cheese by-product and old wine.

Although no longer the action man he once was, when it comes to physical activity the King continues to enjoy fishing and taking long walks in his beloved Highlands. Charles and Camilla's two Jack Russell rescue dogs bring them much joy. The Queen Consort adopted Beth and Bluebell from Battersea Dogs and Cats Home in February 2017, giving them a loving new family. Before being rescued by the charity, Beth was found tied to a post, meanwhile Bluebell was discovered wandering around in the woods with no fur. Previously, before welcoming Beth and Bluebell into their homes, King Charles owned a Jack Russell named Tiger. He died in 2022 and is buried at Highgrove.

Gardening is a passion for both Charles and Camilla. The couple particularly like getting their hands dirty in the organic garden at Highgrove House.

'The garden at Highgrove embodies environmental philosophy - that it is better to work with Nature than against it,' states the Highgrove website.

Charles is a keen advocate of traditional rural skills, is able to lay hedges and has hosted the National Hedgelaying Championships.

For years, the new King has been a keen watercolourist and paints whenever his schedule allows. Lithographs of his paintings have been sold with proceeds going to The Prince of Wales's Charitable Foundation.

'Quite simply, I experienced an overwhelming urge to express what I saw through the medium of watercolour and to convey that almost "inner" sense of texture, which is impossible to achieve via photography,' Charles has said of his love for painting. *'Looking back now at those first sketches, I am appalled by how bad they are. But, nevertheless, the great thing about painting is that you are making your own individual interpretation of whatever view you have chosen. It all requires the most intense concentration and, consequently, is one of the most relaxing and therapeutic exercises I know. In fact, in my case, I find it transports me into another dimension which, quite literally, refreshes parts of the soul which other activities can't reach.'*

The King is also an author, having written, co-written and illustrated several books over the years, beginning with 'The Old Man of Lochnagar', the children's story he penned in 1980 about an old man living in a cave surrounding the corrie loch under the Lochnagar, a mountain which overlooks the royal estate at Balmoral. Other books he has written in the years since include 'A Vision of Britain: A Personal View of Architecture' and 'Rain Forest Lecture'.

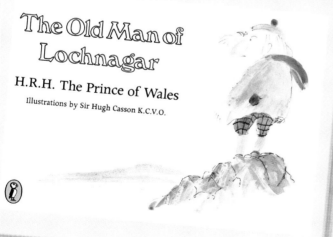

Above:

Prince Charles weeding his herb garden at Highgrove, Gloucestershire in 1986

Left:

'The Old Man of Lochnagar', the children's story Charles wrote in 1980

Below:

Prince Charles's Watercolour paintings were published in a book called HRH The Prince Of Wales Watercolours published in the 1990s. Here is his painting of Balmoral castle

The Perpetual Prince

'The only fit material for a constitutional King is a Prince who begins early to reign'

Walter Bagehot in 'The English Constitution', 1867

Seventy years, two hundred and fourteen days. . . Prince Charles was heir to the throne for longer than any other in British history. The only one to come close to this time scale was Queen Victoria's heir, the future Edward VII, whose own reign as 'King in Waiting' lasted almost 60 years. Victoria guarded her sovereignty jealously, refusing to give Edward, or Bertie as he was known, any responsibility with the result that he frittered away the years gorging on women, gargantuan amounts of food and drink, tobacco and hunting. On many occasions, he voiced his frustration at having so little of value to do. While this certainly isn't the case with his great, great grandson, it is true to say that, at times, during his 70-year wait to ascend the throne, Charles questioned his role as heir, felt his best years were going to waste and even, it has been suggested, pushed for his mother to abdicate.

Right:
The Prince of Wales taken at Buckingham Palace, 1972

The first episode of the fifth series of Netflix's 'The Crown' is entitled 'Queen Victoria Syndrome'. This refers to the phenomenon of a monarch staying on the throne despite being unpopular. The phrase has its roots in the long reign of Queen Victoria who ruled the United Kingdom of Great Britain and Ireland from 1837 until her death in 1901. Royal expert Ingrid Seward characterized her as an '*invisible queen*' after the death of her husband Prince Albert in 1861, after which she became largely reclusive - and stayed that way for the majority of her 63-year-old reign. At various times, there were calls for her to abdicate in favour of Bertie. The scenes in 'The Crown' allude to this syndrome with actor Dominic West's Prince Charles reading aloud a supposed quote from a newspaper article.

Above:

Christening of Charles (centre, wearing the royal christening gown) in 1948: (from left to right) his grandfather King George VI; his mother, Princess Elizabeth, holding him; his father, Philip; and his grandmother Queen Elizabeth

'I declare before you all that my whole life whether it be long or short shall be devoted to your service and the service of our great imperial family to which we all belong'

Princess Elizabeth had proclaimed on her 21st birthday

'Queen Victoria Syndrome? Yes, I saw that,' he says, scanning a copy of the UK's Sunday Times. 'An aging monarch, too long on the throne whose remoteness from the modern world has led people to grow tired not just of her, but of the monarchy itself.'

While these scenes — and also those showing the Prince holding secret meetings with then British Prime Minister John Major in which they discuss the possibility of Queen Elizabeth abdicating so that Charles can take the throne – are based more on fiction than fact, according to royal commentator Sarah Gristwood, by the late 1980s, some Royal insiders were reportedly using 'The Queen Victoria Syndrome' phase to describe Queen Elizabeth's reign.

Left:

HRH Princess Elizabeth on the occasion of her engagement to Philip Mountbatten at Buckingham Palace in London, July 1947

Right:

The Queen, the Duke of Edinburgh, the Duke of Cornwall and Princess Anne, October 1957

'By the end of the decade courtiers had begun to talk about QVS or the Queen Victoria Syndrome, whereby a nation could become tired of an ageing monarch and a parasitic royal family,' she wrote in a 2016 piece for the Huff Post. '*Questions of Elizabeth II's retirement were being mooted as early as 1980.'*

Public support for the Queen's abdication peaked 10 years later when, according to Ipsos MORI stats, almost half of the country

---

Above:

Charles and Diana with US president Ronald Reagan and First Lady Nancy Reagan in November 1985

Left:

Prince Charles pets "Harvey," a retriever, during a September photo session at Balmoral Castle, for release on his 30th birthday, 14th November 1978

---

was keen to see her pass on the reins of power. Meanwhile, Prince Charles was often regarded as searching for a purpose.

'Publicly,' wrote royal writer Anthony Holden in 1988, '*the prince's role was that of a caring and thoughtful man in search of good to do — not merely a prince in search of a role, but a crusader in search of a crusade.'*

As Charles celebrated his 50th birthday in November 1998, speculation was high that he wished for his mother to abdicate and allow him to take over. Indeed, a controversial TV film 'Charles at 50' stated that he would be '*delighted'* if she did so. This forced him to issue a strong statement of denial.

'*I begin to tire of needing to issue denials of false stories about all manner of thoughts which I am alleged to be having,'* he said. '*Some stories are so preposterous that they barely warrant a denial. However, others are both so outrageous and hurtful to my family, to the monarchy and to me personally, that they demand a response.'*

Above:

Charles and his first wife, Diana, with Governor of Queensland Sir James Ramsay (far left) and Lady Ramsay (far right), Brisbane, 1983

Right:

Prince Charles cuts his tiered birthday cake at his 40th Birthday party during the launch of his Prince's Youth Business Trust in Birmingham, England, 11th November 1988

Left:

Prince Charles thanks his mother who organized a party at
Buckingham Palace for his 50th birthday

An investigation was said to be under way into which, if any, of the Prince's advisers had given the documentary-makers a briefing with regards to him being frustrated by his very long wait for the throne. The Prince believed that even if his advisers had given factual information to the London Weekend Television programme, they were not responsible for the abdication story which he described as '*abhorrent*'.

Whether there was any substance to the abdication story remains something of a mystery, however realistically there was never any question of Queen Elizabeth abdicating in favour of Charles — unlike Queen Beatrix of the Netherlands giving up the throne for son and heir, Prince Willem-Alexander in 2013 or King Juan Carlos of Spain making way for his heir, Prince Felipe in 2014. On her 21st birthday, as Princess Elizabeth she had proclaimed. . .

'*I declare before you all that my whole life whether it be long or short shall be devoted to your service and the service of our great imperial family to which we all belong.*'

At the coronation in June 1953, she had anointed Queen.

'*One main reason why the Queen will absolutely not abdicate is unlike other European monarchs, she is an anointed Queen,*' commented royal historian Hugo Vickers, referring to the pact she made with God during her coronation. '*And if you are an anointed Queen, you do not abdicate.*'

Left:

Prince Charles, Prince of Wales holds a birthday cake he was given as he and Camilla, Duchess of Cornwall, visit Beckton Community Centre as part of the launch of The Prince's Trust Youth week on November 14, 2008, Prince Charles 60th Birthday

Right:

The Prince of Wales receives a birthday present and helium balloon for his 70th birthday as he attends an Age UK Tea, celebrating 70 inspirational people marking their 70th birthday in 2018

'Over his 70 years, Philip and I have seen Charles become a champion of conservation and the arts, a great charitable leader and a dedicated and respected heir to the throne to stand comparison with any in history'

Queen Elizabeth II said on the occasion of his 70th birthday

What is even more certain is the Queen's own feelings about calls for abdication, which she made clear in her Christmas broadcast in 1991.

'Next February will see the 40th anniversary of my father's death and of my Accession. Over the years I have tried to follow my father's example and to serve you as best I can,' she told the Commonwealth. 'I feel the same obligation to you that I felt in 1952. With your prayers, and your help, and with the love and support of my family, I shall try to serve you in the years to come.'

The long wait was undeniably difficult for Charles — and uniquely difficult at that. As a son, of course he wanted his mother to live for as long as possible. But as heir to the throne, his raison d'etre — his very destiny - was to inherit said ancient throne.

It has been speculated that Queen Elizabeth felt Charles would not make a good King when his time came but there is no evidence to seriously suggest this. She may have had doubts as to his suitability for kingship during his early years, the troubled days of his first marriage and in the aftermath of an acrimonious separation and divorce but certainly in later years, she could not have been more complimentary.

'Over his 70 years, Philip and I have seen Charles become a champion of conservation and the arts, a great charitable leader and a dedicated and respected heir to the throne to stand comparison with any in history,' she said on the occasion of his 70th birthday.

Then, shortly before her death in September 2022, she again praised her eldest son's King-like qualities.

'For me, there can be no greater pleasure or comfort than to know that into his care are safely-entrusted the guiding principles of public service and duty to others,' she was quoted as saying not long before she passed away in September 2022.

However, in years previous, Charles' confidence must have taken a knock when polls suggested that the public would prefer Prince William to ascend the throne after his grandmother Elizabeth's demise — and in so-doing, by-pass Charles altogether. And then there were those damming words about his suitability as King spoken by Princess Diana during her explosive Panorama interview in 1995.

'Because I know the character,' she said, 'I would think that the

top job, as I call it, would bring enormous limitations to him and I don't know whether he could adapt to that.'

In truth, it hasn't been easy for Charles to adapt and not make his sometimes — very strident — opinions known, a constitutional no-no for the Royals. The 27 'black spider' memos (the 'black spider' allusion referring to his handwriting) sent in 2004 and 2005 attest to that. In these memos, the Prince made direct and persistent policy demands to then British Prime Minister Tony Blair and several key figures in his Labour government. From Blair, Charles demanded everything from urgent action to improve equipment for troops fighting in Iraq to the availability of alternative herbal medicines in the UK. This cache of memos between Prince Charles and senior government ministers were released in 2015 after a 10-year legal battle, offering the clearest picture yet of the breadth and depth of the heir to the throne's lobbying at the highest level of politics.

Above:

Prince Charles Delivering the Queen's Speech on behalf of his mother, May 2022

Despite Charles' misgivings and frustrations at having to wait so long to ascend the throne, the noises he did or didn't make about abdication in 1998, and public opinion seemingly preferring a future William V to Charles III, there was never — bar the monarchy falling in a revolution, that is - any real danger of this longest reigning heir in history failing to fulfil his destiny, take on the role for which he had been born and do it to the best of his abilities.

'If at some stage in the distant future I was to succeed my mama,' he told writer and broadcaster Jonathan Dimbleby in the 1990s, *'then obviously I would do my best to fulfil that role. Sometimes you daydream the sort of things you might do. . .'*

King Charles III

'As the Queen herself did with such unswerving devotion, I, too, now solemnly pledge myself, throughout the remaining time God grants me, to uphold the constitutional principles at the heart of our nation'

King Charles III's first address to the nation on ascending the throne

Although it had been expected within the Royal Family, the death of Queen Elizabeth II still came as a shock — to Prince Charles as much as anyone. The burden of grief hung heavy on his shoulders as he and his sister Princess Anne sat at their mother's bedside as she passed away on the afternoon of September 8 2022. For Charles, though, it was not only grief at losing his *'beloved mama'* that he was dealing with. After a 70 year wait, he was finally King. He may well have felt fear and trepidation at what the future held now he was monarch but the truth is, since that early September day, he has barely put a foot wrong — that's if you excuse his impatience with a spluttering fountain pen in the very early days of his reign!

'Everything His Majesty has done has hit the right tone,' his former communications chief, Kristina Kyriacou, has said. *'Both the King and Queen Consort have just got on with things and are taking care of business. The King has really come across as the elder statesman and seems to have grown in stature. He has always been a fantastic listener and convener. But what we have seen during is him convening everybody in a more statesmanlike way. All the King cares about is serving the British public. He just wants to do the job he sees as his destiny.'*

It certainly seems that Charles has not been afraid to address concerns the public may have had about him — such as meddling in politics and those 'black spider' memos. He has voiced his respect for the constitutional guidelines that come with being monarch, emphasised the importance of living in a multicultural world and promoted religious tolerance. However, he is very well aware that as King, he must abide by the constitution.

Right:

Prince Charles, Queen Elizabeth, and Prince Edward are shown here on the lawn of their Windsor home, 01 April, 1969

Above:

King Charles III during a reception with Realm
High Commissioners and their spouses in the Bow
Room at Buckingham Palace on September 11, 2022
in London, England. King Charles III ascended the throne
of the United Kingdom on the death of his mother, Queen
Elizabeth II on 8 September 2022

'I do realise that it is a separate exercise being sovereign, so of course I understand entirely how that should operate,' he told the BBC in 2018. *'You can't be the same as the sovereign if you're the Prince of Wales or the heir. But the idea somehow that I'm going to go on in exactly the same way if I have to succeed, is complete nonsense because the two situations are completely different.'*

Charles plans to keep the 'hardy annuals' of the royal calendar – such as Royal Ascot, the garden parties and the Maundy Service — but it remains to be seen how far he takes his eco-activism now he sits on the throne. However, he will be conscious of his choices and will push for environmental sustainability.

'He's very much trying to create a new global platform for the British monarchy,' says historian Ed Owens.

Charles intends to 'slim down' the monarchy so that the 'firm' compromises of seven people — himself, Camilla, the new Prince and Princess of Wales, Prince Edward and Sophie, Countess of Wessex, and Princess Anne, the Princess Royal. With regards to the Duke and Duchess of Sussex, Charles mentioned them in his first speech as sovereign but has not allowed them and their controversial media projects to become a distraction. His Sussex grandchildren, Archie and Lilibet, are entitled to be ennobled now their grandfather is King but that issue is very much on the back burner.

Right top:

Memorials inside Tottenham Court Road station marking the death of Queen Elizabeth II

Middle:

The gate in front of the Queen's Sandringham Residence in Norfolk

Bottom:

The funeral procession for Queen Elizabeth II

Left:

King Charles III and Camilla, Queen Consort during a State Banquet at Buckingham Palace on November 22, 2022

'Anything to do with his grandchildren will be decided once Harry and Meghan stop lobbing salvos into the palace,' says one royal insider. 'No decision or pronouncement can be made on that issue until the King is confident that the decision he makes can withstand any activity on either side in the long term – and they are not in that place right now. Monarchs move with great caution and reflection and there is no obligation to rush. The King will, of course, need to make a decision at some point – but the Sussexes' activity is still so changeable that it's just hard to take any firm decisions at this stage.'

At 73 years old when most of us are actively slowing down, Charles — and 75-year-old, Camilla — have taken on challenging new roles — demanding both mentally and physically. However, they know they must pace themselves and for them, this means continuing (whenever possible) with the lifestyle they enjoyed before they became King and Queen Consort.

'They genuinely have a wonderful relationship and make a great team, but they don't live in each other's pockets,' says a family friend.

So, it comes as no surprise to learn that Charles will continue to use his own home — Highgrove, while Camilla's Wiltshire home, Ray Mill, will continue to be a bolt hole where she can relax with her children and grandchildren. It's said that they regard Birkhall on the Balmoral estate as their marital home. The couple will, of course, spend time at official Royal residences Windsor, Sandringham and Clarence House. With regards to Monarch HQ Buckingham Palace, it has been reported that Charles wishes to minimise the living arrangements there from 50-plus rooms to a single apartment.

'It will be a much more modest flat-above-the-shop situation akin to that of the Prime Minister at 10 Downing Street,' says a source close to the throne. 'The new King wants to change the function of all of the royal residences to ensure they deliver something for the public beyond just being somewhere for members of the royal family to live.'

According to royal watcher Sally Bedell Smith, Charles *'won't really be king (in his mind) until he's consecrated with the holy oil, makes the sacred oath and has the crown on his head. That moment when he is a "transcendent being" in a way, is really, really crucial.'*

The coronation takes place on May 6 2023 (incidentally the fourth birthday of his grandson Archie). It has been reported that the Sussex family have been invited — as they are to all family events. Whether they will come is another matter. However, there is no doubt that our first Coronation for 70 years will be spectacular. Although a low-key ceremony was mooted soon after Charles ascended the throne, public reaction to the late Queen's Platinum Jubilee celebrations and her funeral suggest that the nation expect nothing less than a day big on pageantry.

'The King and Queen Consort and their advisers are keenly following the debate to ensure they are striking the right balance between this moment of celebration and something that can be done against a very challenging economic backdrop,' says a source close to both the Royal Family and the Government. 'Lest we forget, the late Queen's Coronation in 1953 was also a time of great austerity and economic difficulties. So, it's not the first time that the family have had to marry the concerns of the nation with the opportunity the Coronation brings. The Government is keen for it to be a great moment of national celebration because these events of 2022 were a fabulous advertisement for Britain. We do pomp and pageantry in a way that no other nation can.'

God Save Our Gracious King,
Long Live Our Noble King,
God Save The King!

Above:

King Charles III and Camilla, Queen Consort attend the Christmas
Day service at St Mary Magdalene Church on December 25, 2022
in Sandringham, Norfolk. King Charles III ascended to the throne on
September 8, 2022, with his coronation set for May 6, 2023

To Play a Prince

How King Charles III has been portrayed on stage and screen...

1992

The late actor Roger Rees portrayed Prince Charles opposite Catherine Oxenberg's Princess Diana in the 1992 television movie 'Charles and Diana: Unhappily Ever After'. The film received dismal reviews.

1993

David Threlfall played Prince Charles to Serena Scott Thomas's Princess Diana in the 1993 TV movie 'Diana: Her True Story', which is based on the book of the same name by British journalist Andrew Morton. At the time, Entertainment Weekly raved about David's performance, writing, *'Charles … has found his dead ringer in David Threlfall. Threlfall has a horsey, long-jawed face that is similar in shape to the Prince's, but the actor has brought his own witty technique to the role: not merely stiffening his upper lip but freezing it, while constantly chewing on the lower one, with the result that Charles' upper-class-twit voice always sounds faintly strangled and agonized'.*

1996

'Princess in Love' hit the small screen with Christopher Bowen playing Prince Charles. The television film focused less on Princess Diana's unhappy marriage to the future monarch and more on her affair and romance with Captain James Hewitt – and it was actually based on a book of the same name to which the handsome British army officer contributed.

2006

Alex Jennings' made his breakthrough film role as Charles, Prince of Wales opposite Helen Mirren's Queen Elizabeth II in Oscar-winning film 'The Queen'.

2011

The Hallmark Channel brought Prince William and Princess Kate's love story to the small screen with 'William and Catherine: A Royal Romance'. Actor Victor Garber took on the role of Prince Charles in the 2011 flick. At the time, he told 'People' magazine about a big similarity he shares with the current king, quipping, 'I'm playing Prince Charles, of course – we have the same ears.'

Ben Cross portrayed Prince Charles in Lifetime's take on Prince William and Duchess Kate's romance in TV movie 'William and Kate'.

2014

Late actor Tim Pigott-Smith played a post-accession Prince Charles in play 'King Charles III' for which he received a nomination for the Olivier Award for Best Actor and a Tony Award nomination for the play's production on Broadway. He also appeared as Charles in the 2017 film adaptation of the play.

Below:

The original West End and Broadway poster for King Charles III

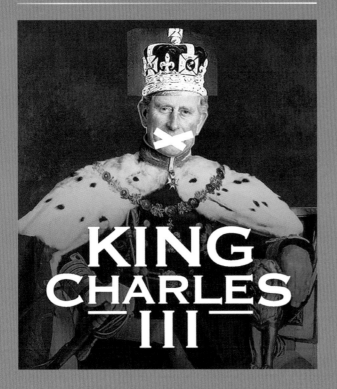

2016

Billy Jenkins played a young Prince Charles on season one of 'The Crown'.

2017

Julian Baring played a school-aged Prince Charles on season two of 'The Crown'.

2018

Steve Coulter took on the role of Prince Charles in the 2018 Lifetime television movie 'Harry & Meghan: A Royal Romance,' which fictionalized the love story of Prince Harry and Duchess Meghan.

2019

Josh O'Connor played an adult Prince Charles on seasons three and four of 'The Crown'. He opened up about playing the Royal to 'Screen Daily', saying, *'We all have a set position on the dynamic between Charles and Diana. It's been great to have the ability to either fight against that or, at times, acknowledge it and also to challenge any question of, "Did he ever love her?" Personally I think he must have done. There's a wealth of layers and richness to Charles and Diana, and I loved seeking that out.'* It paid off: In 2021, Josh won best actor in a drama series at the Emmys for his performance.

2021

Princess Diana's story got the Broadway treatment with 'Diana: The Musical'. Roe Hartrampf played the role of Prince Charles. *'One thing I learned about Prince Charles that I wasn't expecting is about his humanity – what a good person he is at his core,'* Roe told 'Broadway.com'. *'I think that having maybe some of the worst years of his life play out so openly in the media gives us a certain impression of him. It's part of my job to strip away those preconceived notions and try and find the human being at the centre of this character.'*

Kristen Stewart famously tackled the role of Princess Diana in the film 'Spencer' with actor Jack Farthing serving as her Prince Charles. He was nervous to take the part, telling 'Insider', *'It's obviously a very scary overwhelming idea, taking on someone like that. Trying to find your own truth in a character that everyone knows so well and is so visible and so recorded and so impersonated.'*

2022

Dominic West portrays Prince Charles on seasons five and six of 'The Crown', season six being released in November 2023. In an interview with Netflix, Dominic admitted *he* only saw similarities between himself and the current king from a very specific angle. *'The only time I really look like Charles is from behind. 'Cause the hair is just perfect.'*

A King Crowned

'The things which I have here before promised,
I will perform and keep. So help me God'

Coronation oath of King Charles III,
May 6 2023

The coronation of Queen Elizabeth II which took place on June 2 1953 was a three-hour affair from start to finish. Glorious though it had undoubtedly been, King Charles III instinctively felt that a carbon copy of his mother's crowning would no longer be appropriate in a much-changed United Kingdom seven decades on. After lengthy discussions, His Majesty and his coronation committee, made up of privy counsellors and headed by The Duke of Norfolk, Edward Fitzalan-Howard, decided which elements to keep and which to change. It was agreed that the ceremony itself should be shortened by an hour and the guest list slashed from the 8,000 who had attended the late Queen's Coronation to around 2,200. It was also decided to make the King's procession notably shorter than the five-mile route taken by Elizabeth II from Westminster Abbey back to Buckingham Palace in 1953. The King would not replicate his mother's journey which had wound its way along Regent Street, Oxford Street and Park Lane, but would instead return to Buckingham Palace via Whitehall, Admiralty Arch and The Mall. However, it was proposed that the pomp and pageantry — for which Britain is world famous - would still be on display in all its glory.

With the date set for May 6 2023, the invitations went out to the lucky guests in early April. The invites themselves were exquisite and a riot of floral colour. Designed by renowned heraldic

WESTMINSTER ABBEY

THE CORONATION OF
THEIR MAJESTIES

KING CHARLES III
AND
QUEEN CAMILLA

Saturday, 6th May, 2023
at 11.00 a.m.

Above:

Official programme for the day

Right:

Official invitation, designed by Andrew Jamieson

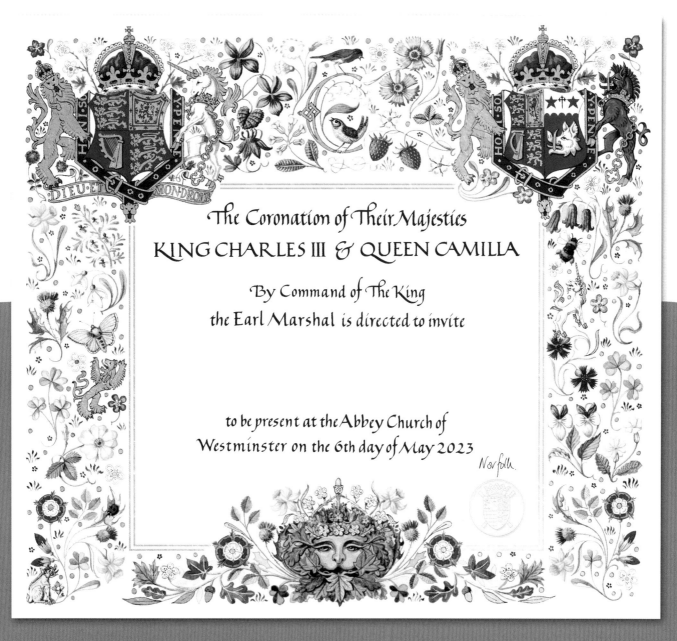

The Coronation of Their Majesties
KING CHARLES III & QUEEN CAMILLA

By Command of The King
the Earl Marshal is directed to invite

to be present at the Abbey Church of
Westminster on the 6th day of May 2023

Norfolk.

artist and manuscript illuminator Andrew Jamieson, the British wildflowers depicted featured lily of the valley, cornflowers, wild strawberries, dog roses, bluebells, and a sprig of rosemary for remembrance, together with wildlife including a bee, a butterfly, a ladybird, a wren and a robin. Flowers appeared in groupings of three, signifying the King becoming the third monarch of his name. The invitation also included the motif of the Green Man, an ancient figure from British folklore, symbolic of spring and rebirth. What could be more fitting to celebrate a May coronation and the new reign of a King for whom nature is a passion?

As the date drew ever closer, London and the United Kingdom as a whole prepared itself for the Big Day. In addition to the ceremony itself, an outdoors extravaganza of a concert at Windsor was planned for the evening of Sunday May 7, the day after the coronation. It was also proposed that volunteering and all manner of good works within communities take place on bank holiday Monday May 8. Preparations were made for street parties to be thrown up and down the land over the long weekend.

The week before the coronation, Royal enthusiasts started to

Main Image

King Charles III travelling in the Diamond Jubilee Coach along the Mall from Buckingham Palace on route to Westminster Abbey for the Coronation of King Charles III and Queen Camilla on May 06, 2023 in London, England.

Bottom Right:

Some of the Armed Forces that escorted the Diamond Jubilee Coach.

camp out on the Mall, eager to secure the best views for the celebrations and procession. Following a surprise appearance from the King and the Prince and Princess of Wales on the Mall to meet the crowds on coronation eve, the procession formally began at 10.20am on May 6 when Charles and Camilla departed Buckingham Palace in the Diamond Jubilee State Coach, drawn by six Windsor Greys. They were accompanied by the Sovereign's Escort of the Household Cavalry Mounted Regiment. It was raining — just as it had at Elizabeth II's coronation - but nothing could dampen the enthusiasm of the assembled crowds and well-wishers. The coronation ceremony began at 11am with the procession into the abbey led by leaders and representatives from non-Christian religions, including the Buddhist, Hindu, Jain, Jewish, Muslim and Sikh communities. They were followed by Christian leaders from different Christian denominations, including the Church of England. After this, the flags of the Commonwealth realms were carried by representatives, accompanied by their governors general and prime ministers. Charles and Camilla formed their own procession, led by four peers who carried heraldic standards. The soon-to-be crowned

King and Queen were each attended by four pages of honour while Camilla was also accompanied by two ladies in attendance - her sister, Annabel Elliot, and close friend, the Marchioness of Lansdowne. The choir sang Hubert Parry's 'I Was Glad', written for the coronation of King Edward VII in 1902, during which the King's Scholars of Westminster School sang 'Vivat Regina Camilla' ('Long live Queen Camilla') and 'Vivat Rex Carolus' (Long live King Charles). The coronation regalia for both the King and Queen was then processed to the altar. On arrival at the altar, the King was addressed by a young chorister of the Chapel Royal.

'Your Majesty, as children of the Kingdom of God we welcome you in the name of the King of Kings,' came the greeting.

'In His name and after His example, I come not to be served but to serve,' replied King Charles.

There followed a moment of silent prayer before the King and Queen took their seats on the chairs of estate. These had been made for Queen Elizabeth II and Prince Philip but were

Left Top:

King Charles III arrives for his coronation with Queen Camilla at Westminster Abbey on May 6, 2023 in London, England.

Left Bottom:

King Charles III with the St Edward's Crown on his head attends the Coronation Ceremony inside Westminster Abbey in central London on May 6, 2023.

reupholstered and hand embroidered with the cyphers of the new King and Queen Consort for this coronation. Archbishop of Canterbury, Justin Welby, gave the greeting and introduction before the Kyrie Eleison - an ancient prayer first canted at the beginning of the Holy Communion about 1600 years ago — was sung. For the first time at a coronation, it was sung in the Welsh language and performed by bass-baritone, Sir Bryn Terfel. Following this emotional and rousing rendition, the Archbishop of Canterbury — together with Lady Angiolini representing the Order of the Thistle, Christopher Finney chair of the Victoria Cross and George Cross Association and representing recipients of bravery medals, and Baroness Amos representing the Order of the Garter — stood facing north, south, east and west respectively and, in turn, asked the congregation to recognise Charles as King.

'I here present unto you King Charles, your undoubted King,' each repeated, one after the other. *'Each wherefore all you who are come this day to do your homage and service. Are you willing to do the same?'*

The congregation replied *'God save King Charles!'* after each pronouncement. Charles was then presented with a new Bible by the Moderator of the General Assembly of the Church of Scotland.

Before administering the oath, the Archbishop of Canterbury acknowledged the existence of multiple faiths and beliefs in the United Kingdom. Charles then took the coronation oath whereby he swore to govern each of his countries according to their respective laws and customs, to administer law and justice with mercy, to uphold Protestantism in the United Kingdom and protect the Church of England. He proceeded to the altar and stated, *'The things which I have here before promised I will perform and keep. So, help me God.'*

The service of Holy Communion then followed. The Archbishop of Canterbury recited the Collect prayer before the Epistle and Gospel were read by Prime Minister, Rishi Sunak, and the Bishop of London, Sarah Mullally, respectively. The Archbishop of Canterbury's sermon followed. Then came the most sacred part of the coronation — the anointing of King Charles III with holy oil sourced from two groves on the Mount of Olives overlooking Jerusalem — those of the Monastery of Mary Magdalene and the Monastery of the Ascension. The oil had then been consecrated by the patriarch of Jerusalem and the Anglican archbishop in Jerusalem. For the oath, Charles removed his robe of state and sat on the ancient coronation chair, known as King Edward's Chair, which dates back to 1296 and has been used at every coronation since 1308. The Stone of Scone, an ancient sandstone slab upon which the Kings of Scotland were inaugurated, had been brought from Edinburgh Castle for the occasion and placed inside the bottom of the chair. As the choir sang Handel's anthem 'Zadok the Priest' which the German composer had written for the 1727 coronation of King George II, the anointing screens were moved into place by troops from the Household Division. Away from view, the oil was poured from the 17th century golden ampulla or flask, and the King was anointed using a medieval spoon, the most ancient item of the coronation regalia. Assisted by the Archbishop of York and Dean of Westminster, the Archbishop of Canterbury anointed the King on his hands, chest and head, making the shape of the cross. As the screens were removed, Charles knelt before the high altar as the Archbishop of Canterbury gave a blessing. More ancient symbolism followed as the King was dressed in the coronation robes - the Colobium Sindonis, a sleeveless white linen garment symbolising purity and simplicity; the supertunica, an elaborately embroidered gold coat; and the sword belt - or girdle. All these items had been used in previous coronations, with the supertunica worn by King George V, King George VI and Queen Elizabeth II, and the sword belt used by King George VI.

After the coronation robes came the Crown Jewels (normally kept at the Tower of London) and the coronation regalia, presented to the King by peers from the House of Lords and senior bishops. The first item of regalia was the spurs, representing knighthood and chivalry. These were brought to the King to acknowledge by the Lord Great Chamberlain and then returned to the altar. He next received the jewelled sword from the lord president of the Privy Council, Penny Mordaunt MP, as the Archbishop of Canterbury read a prayer. Ms Mordaunt then 'redeemed' the sword by offering a small velvet bag of coins, containing 100 newly-minted 50p pieces featuring the King's image. During this practice, a Greek Orthodox chant was sung in memory of the King's father, Prince Philip, who was born a Prince of Greece. The King next received and acknowledged the gold armills or bracelets, representing sincerity and wisdom, presented by Lord Kamal . Prince William then helped present his father with the stole royal - a long, narrow length of cloth worn around the neck, and the imperial mantle - a long gold-coloured robe. Next up was the golden orb, representing the sovereign's power and symbolising the world under the cross of Christ which the Archbishop of Canterbury placed in the King's right hand. Then came the monarch's ring, presented by Lord Patel. The King acknowledged it before it was returned to the altar, with the Archbishop announcing that it was a *'sign of the covenant sworn this day between God and King, King and people'*. The coronation glove was then presented by Lord Singh of Wimbledon, with the King placing it on his right hand as a symbol of the sovereign as advocate and challenger for the protection and honour of the people. The sceptre with cross and rod with dove were the final items handed to the King before the crowning.

The pinnacle of the ceremony had arrived - the crowning of King Charles III. The Dean of Westminster handed St Edward's crown to the Archbishop of Canterbury who said a prayer of blessing before placing it on the King's head and proclaiming, *'God save the King'* with the congregation echoing his words. The bells of Westminster Abbey rang out for two minutes in addition to fanfares and gun salutes fired from Horse Guards Parade, the Tower of London, and at saluting stations across the UK - as well as from ships at sea.

A blessing by church figures from across the UK followed with the Archbishop of Canterbury leading the words of fealty to the King on behalf of the Church as he promised to be faithful and true to his monarch. Historically these homages had great significance in maintaining law and order. The King moved to his throne, originally made for his grandfather George VI in 1937, and there followed one of the most touching moments of the entire ceremony. Prince William knelt before his father proclaiming, *'I, William, Prince of Wales, pledge my loyalty to you and faith and truth I will bear unto you, as your liege man of life and limb. So, help me God.'* Prince William touched his father's crown before kissing him on the cheek.

The King, visibly moved, replied with a heartfelt, *'Thank you William.'*

The congregation - and people around the UK and Commonwealth - were then invited to participate in public homage with the words, *'I swear that I will pay true allegiance to Your Majesty, and to your heirs and successors according to law. So, help me God.'*

The King's crowning finished with the anthem 'Confortare' by Sir Walford-Davies.

Attention now fell on Queen Consort Camilla, who would receive her own glittering regalia before being crowned — the last consort to be crowned having been the Queen Mother in 1937. It is a ceremony that only female consorts receive - hence there was no such ritual for Prince Philip in 1953. Unlike the King, no privacy screen was used for Camilla's crowning. The Archbishop marked her head with holy oil, saying: *'Almighty God, the fountain of all goodness; hear our prayer this day for thy servant Camilla, whom in thy name, and with all devotion, we consecrate our Queen.'*

Right:

Queen Camilla departs the Coronation service of King Charles III and Queen Camilla at Westminster Abbey on May 06, 2023 in London, England.

She was presented with the consort's ring before the Dean of Westminster handed the crown, made for Queen Mary at the time of her and George V's coronation in 1911, to the Archbishop. In tribute to Queen Elizabeth II, the crown had been reset with the Cullinan diamonds, gems that the late Queen often wore as brooches and were said to be known within the Royal Family as 'Granny's Chips'. Queen Camilla was then presented with a sceptre and the rod of 'equity and mercy' by the Bishop of Dover and Lord Chartres.

A coronation anthem by Lord Andrew Lloyd Webber, based on verses from Psalm 98, was performed as Queen Camilla took her place in her own throne chair beside the King. After another hymn, the couple removed their crowns, returning to the chairs of estate as holy communion took place. Before leaving the Abbey, the King and Queen headed to the Chapel of St Edward, behind the high altar, to put on their robes of estate with His Majesty also putting on the Imperial State Crown. Following this, there was a final blessing before the congregation joined in with a rendition of the national anthem. The King and Queen and their respective retinues then made their way slowly back down the aisle to the accompaniment of Elgar's Pomp and Circumstance March No.4, the congregation bowing their heads or curtseying as they passed. At the door, the King and Queen received a greeting from leaders and representatives of the Jewish, Hindu, Sikh, Muslim and Buddhist faiths.

Their Majesties returned from Westminster Abbey to Buckingham Palace in the Gold State Coach, built for the coronation of George III in 1727. This magnificent but highly uncomfortable vehicle was drawn by eight Windsor Grey horses, with other members of the royal family following in other horse-drawn coaches or by limousine. The second procession followed the same route as the first, but in reverse and on a larger scale. The armed forces of the United Kingdom, the Commonwealth, and the British Overseas Territories played a significant part. Over 5,000 members of the British Armed Forces and 400 Armed Forces personnel from at least 35 other Commonwealth countries were part of the procession, and 1,000 lined the route.

On arrival at Buckingham Palace, the King and Queen received a royal salute and three cheers from armed forces personnel who were massed in palace gardens. Their Majesties then appeared on the famous balcony of Buckingham Palace, joined by their attendants and other family members, most notably the Prince and Princess of Wales and their children George, Charlotte and Louis. They waved to the teaming crowds below before enjoying the spectacle of a flypast by helicopters and the Red Arrows aerobatic team. It had truly been a day to remember.

God Save The King!

Right:

King Charles III and Queen Camilla travelling in the Gold State Coach built in 1760 and used at every Coronation since that of William IV in 1831 travels down The Mall on route to Buckingham Palace during the Coronation of King Charles III and Queen Camilla on May 06, 2023 in London, England

Above:

Buckingham Palace balcony during the Coronation of King Charles
III and Queen Camilla on May 06, 2023 in London, England. The
Coronation of Charles III and his wife, Camilla.

Coronation Couture

*Queen Camilla

Designed by Bruce Oldfield, Her Majesty's Coronation gown was a regal white coat dress in silk with an embroidered underskirt underneath. Exquisitely embroidered onto the garment were the names of her two children and five grandchildren. Images of the King and Queen's beloved rescue Jack Russell terriers, Beth and Bluebell, were embroidered just above the hem of the gown, their distinctive profiles rendered in gold thread. Further embroidery featured Camilla's Royal Cipher and the flower emblems from the United Kingdom's four nations - English rose, Scots thistle, Welsh daffodil and the shamrock of Northern Ireland. She wore the necklace and earrings made for Queen Victoria at her coronation in 1837. Queen Camilla wore two separate mantles. On arrival at Westminster Abbey, she sported the crimson, ermine-trimmed cloak made for the late Queen Elizabeth II who wore it at her 1953 coronation. On departing the Abbey, the newly crowned Queen wore a new mantle in majestic, purple velvet.

*The Princess of Wales and Princess Charlotte

Alexander McQueen, Catherine's go-to couturier for big occasions, designed her coronation gown in ivory silk crepe and also the cape dress of eight-year-old Charlotte. The matching dresses were embroidered with rose, shamrock, daffodil and thistle motifs to signify the four nations, and mother and daughter wore matching silver headpieces created by the milliner Jess Collett. In a tribute to her late mother-in-law, Catherine wore pearl and diamond earrings that had belonged to Diana. Over her gown the Princess of Wales wore the mantle of the Royal Victorian Order.

*Sophie, Duchess of Edinburgh

A stunning white Suzannah London gown was worn by Sophie, the Duchess of Edinburgh to the coronation. Featuring lace applique at the collar and made from a sustainable crepe fabric, the dress and train were intricately embroidered with representations of British meadow flowers, using a traditional Irish technique. In line with the Princess of Wales' attire, the Duchess of Edinburgh also donned a blue and red mantle over her gown - a nod to the colours of the union jack.

*Penny Mordaunt

In her self-designed teal dress and cape, made by Safiyaa, and matching headband with both featuring a gold fern embroidery, Conservative politician Penny Mordaunt, who was responsible for carrying the sword of state and offering to the king, is widely acknowledged to have stolen the sartorial show at the coronation. This was the first time the role of sword bearer had been carried out by a woman and Mordaunt had wanted an outfit specifically designed for a woman, rather than the standard black-and-gold court dress usually worn. She also paid for the stunning ensemble herself.

*Carol Middleton and Pippa Middleton Matthews

The Princess of Wales' mother wore Catherine Walker to the 2011 wedding of her elder daughter and Prince William, and did so again for the coronation. She looked uber-stylish in her CW coat dress in cobalt blue with matching headband. Younger Middleton daughter, Pippa, oozed understated sophistication in her soft lemon yellow coat dress by Claire Mischevani for the occasion. A bespoke hat by Jane Taylor London proved the perfect finishing touch.

*Queen Letizia of Spain

The Spanish queen wowed the crowds in a bubble-gum pink dress by Carolina Herrera which featured a long-sleeve top with peplum detailing, intricate lace panels, button-down detailing, long sleeves, and a matching midi skirt. The elegant and eye-catching look was topped off with a statement, wide-brimmed hat.

cuffs, with an open-fronted design. An ivory silk satin waistcoat trimmed in gold braid, wool trousers and boots completed the outfit.

*Dr Jill Biden and granddaughter Finnegan Biden

The FLOTUS and her granddaughter made a stylishly political statement with their choice of couture for the coronation in which they showed their support for Ukraine by dressing in the colours of the Ukirianian flag. Dr Biden donned a vibrant blue Ralph Lauren two-piece suit set while Finnegan opted for a pastel yellow Markarian midi dress.

*Nicholas Barclay

Nicholas (13) is the son of solicitor Piers Barclay and Rose Troughton, a scion of the Colman mustard dynasty and goddaughter to King Charles as well as a descendant of the 14th Earl of Strathmore and Kinghorne. Rose's mother is Sarah Troughton, a close friend of Queen Camilla, second cousin to the King, and the first female Lord Lieutenant of Wiltshire.

*Brigitte Macron

The First Lady of France wore Louis Vuitton — an immaculate pastel pink ensemble consisting of a knee-length shift dress and a military-style coat with buttons.

*Lord Oliver Cholmondeley

The 13-year-old younger son of the seventh Marquess of Cholmondeley and his wife, Lady Rose — the family are neighbours and friends of the King and Queen in Norfolk, living at Houghton Hall close to the Sandringham estate.

His n Her Pages

The King and Queen were accompanied by eight exquisitely dressed and well-behaved page boys — four each - as they entered and departed Westminster Abbey. Historically, pages were chosen purely for their pedigree but in 2023, family and friendship take precedence.

*Ralph Tollemache

Ralph (12) is the son of the Hon Edward and Sophia Tollemache. Edward, a banker, is a godson of King Charles, and Sophia is a friend of Princess Eugenie.

King Charles's Retinue

*Prince George

Nine-year-old grandson of the King and second in line to the throne after his father William, the young Prince, like his three fellow pages, wore a copy of a uniform first seen at the Coronation of Edward VII in 1902. It comprised a scarlet tunic, decorated with gold lace trim and blue velvet

Queen Camilla's Retinue

*Louis Lopes

The Queen's grandson, Louis (13) wore a red uniform based on those of the Grenadier Guards, of which his granny is Colonel-in-Chief. Louis is one of twins, sons of the Queen's daughter, art curator Laura, and her husband, Harry Lopes, a former model turned eco-entrepreneur.

*Gus Lopes

Louis's twin was dressed in uniform reminiscent of the Rifles, of which the Queen is also Colonel-in-Chief, Gus wore a green jacket featuring red Rifles piping, with an historic collar braid on the neck and front, and Her Majesty's cypher on the shoulder.

*Freddy Parker Bowles

Dressed like his cousin Louis, Freddy (13) is the son of food writer Tom Parker Bowles — Camilla's son and godson to the King — and his former wife Sara Buys, a fashion editor. A dedicated Tottenham Hotspurs football supporter, Freddy wore the team's socks under his trousers at the coronation.

*Arthur Elliot

A grand-nephew to the Queen, Arthur (10) is the son of her nephew Ben Elliot and his wife, Mary-Clare Winwood, US-born daughter of the musician Steve Winwood. Arthur wore the Rifles uniform like his cousin, Gus.

Coronation Jewels & Regalia

*St Edward Crown

Crafted in 1661 for King Charles II, the previous Crown jewels having been destroyed during Oliver Cromwell's republic. The crown was resized specifically for Charles III in December 2022. Cast in solid gold, it is covered in more than 400 precious and semi-precious stones, including rubies, sapphires, garnets, topazes, tourmalines and amethysts. It is estimated to be worth around £4 billion. Weighing 2.2 kilos, it is the crown Charles III was crowned with.

*The Imperial State Crown

Worn by Charles at the close of the coronation. It is the crown regularly worn by British monarchs at the State Opening of Parliament. Weighing one kg, it was made for the coronation of Charles' grandfather George VI in 1937. It is set with 2,868 diamonds in silver mounts including the 105-carat Cullinan II, the second biggest stone cut from the Cullinan Diamond, which was given by the government of the Transvaal in South Africa to Edward VII on his birthday in 1907. The crown also features the large 'Black Prince's Ruby' along with 17 sapphires, 11 emeralds and 269 pearls, including some of which are said to have been bought as earrings by Tudor monarch Queen Elizabeth I. It is estimated to be worth between £3-5 billion.

*Queen Mary's Crown

Made in 1911 for Queen Mary, consort of King George V, the great grandparents of Charles III. In the interests of sustainability and efficiency, it is the first time in recent history that an existing crown has been used for the coronation of a consort instead of a new commission being made. The controversial Koh-i-Nur diamond was replaced for the coronation and reset with the Cullinan III, IV and V diamonds. The diamonds were part of Queen Elizabeth II's personal jewellery collection for many years and were often worn by Her late Majesty as brooches. Queen Mary's Crown has an estimated value of £400 million.

*Sovereign's Sceptre with Cross

The Cullinan 1 diamond, also known as the Star of Africa, which weighs in at 530 carats and is the world's largest colourless cut diamond, was set in the bejewelled golden sceptre which has been used in every coronation since 1661.The sceptre, which has undergone a number of alterations over the centuries, represents the sovereign's temporal power and is associated with good governance.

*Sovereign's Sceptre with Dove

Also dating from 1661, the second sceptre used in the ceremony represents the sovereign's spiritual role. It is made from a gold rod in three sections, mounted with diamonds, rubies, emeralds, sapphires and spinels. At the top is an enamelled dove with outspread wings, which represents the Holy Ghost.

*Sovereign's Orb

The Sovereign's Orb, another item commissioned for Charles II's coronation, is a globe of gold with a cross mounted on top, surrounded by a band of diamonds, emeralds, rubies, sapphires and pearls with a large amethyst at the summit. It is a representation of Christian sovereignty.

*Coronation Ring

The coronation ring, known as 'The Wedding Ring of England' and composed of a sapphire with a ruby cross set in diamonds, was made for the coronation of King William IV in 1831. Worn at every coronation since then, it symbolises kingly dignity.

*Swords and Maces

A number of swords featured in the coronation procession. These include the Sword of State, which symbolises royal authority and was made in about 1678, and was used at Charles' investiture as Prince of Wales in 1969. Also featured were the Sword of Temporal Justice, the Sword of Spiritual Justice and the Sword of Mercy, which were first used during the coronation of Charles I in 1626.

The bejewelled Sword of Offering, made for the coronation of George IV in 1821, was presented to Charles, with the message of being a symbol not of might or violence but for the protection of good.

Two maces, made of silver gilt over oak and date from between 1660 and 1695, also featured. These are the ceremonial emblems of authority which are carried before the sovereign at events such as the State Opening of Parliament.

*Ampulla

The golden ampulla, which dates from 1661, is a flask in the shape of an eagle that holds the holy oil consecrated in Jerusalem.

*Coronation Spoon

The silver-gilt spoon is the oldest piece in the regalia, probably made for Henry II or Richard I in the 12th century. It was used to anoint King James 1 in 1603 and has featured at every coronation since.

*Bracelets

Two armills - golden bracelets representing sincerity and wisdom, decorated with national emblems of roses, thistles and harps, and lined in red velvet. The armills are thought to relate to ancient symbols of knighthood and military leadership. New armills were specially prepared for Queen Elizabeth's coronation in 1953.

The Coronation in Numbers

2.2: the weight — in kilos - of the St Edwards Crown which was placed on King Charles' head as he was crowned. Created in 1661 for King Charles II, it was resized specifically for Charles III in December 2022.

12: the number of new pieces of music commissioned or selected by the King for the coronation ceremony.

13: the amount of gun salutes from military bases in all four corners of the country and on His Majesty's ships at sea which sounded out the moment the King was crowned.

40: King Charles was the 40th monarch to be crowned at Westminster Abbey.

62: the number of rounds fired at the Tower of London and Horseguards' Parade to mark the coronation.

105: the number of loose diamonds the Princess of Wales wore around her neck during the coronation ceremony, including the George VI festoon necklace, which was made up from diamonds that once belonged to Prince William's great, great-grandmother, Queen Mary.

2200: the amount of diamonds on Camilla's Queen Mary's Crown.

2200: also the number of guests invited to Westminster Abbey for Charles' coronation — approximately a quarter of the number of guests Queen Elizabeth II shoehorned into the venue for her 1953 coronation

6000: the number of armed forces personnel on duty on May 6 2023

100 Million: the estimated cost of the coronation in pounds sterling

300 Million: the number of people who tuned in to watch the coronation around the world

Right:
King Charles III wearing the Imperial state Crown carrying the Sovereign's Orb and Sceptre leaves Westminster Abbey after the Coronation Ceremonies in central London on May 6, 2023.